7-Figure Golf Coaching Blue Print

HOW I BUILT A $1,000,000 Per Year Golf Coaching Business From Scratch (And You Can Too)

By Eric Cogorno

Acknowledgements

I want to thank everyone who made this book possible!

To Mary for all of the help putting this together and being an awesome business partner.

To My Mom for working 3 jobs and doing whatever it took to allow me to pursue my golf dreams. For being my best friend my entire life and showing me what unconditional love looks like.

To Paul for giving me chance after chance after chance.....and paving the way for me to not only get into coaching but serving as an incredible mentor along the way.

And to Paula for making my world go round and allowing me to live out my dream life everyday. I don't know where I would be without you.

I love and appreciate you all!

The goal of this book is to give you a blueprint to follow to build your own 7 figure coaching business.

If you're a coach or someone who sells your services I want this to be your GUIDE to building the business (and ultimately) the lifestyle of your dreams.

I'm going to guide you through step by step what I did to build my 7 figure golf coaching business.

I'll tell you some stories and hopefully give you some memorable nuggets but the MAIN goal of mine is to give you REAL TACTICS to follow.

I've been fortunate to build a coaching business from $0 to over $1,000,000 per year of profit over the past decade.

My coaching revenue looked something like this:

- Year 1: $0-$7,500 (in person only) (part time)
- Year 2: $7,500-$15,000 (in person only) (part time)
- Year 3: $15,000-$30,000 (in person only) (part time)
- Year 4: $30,000-$60,000 (in person only)
- Year 5: $60,000-$80,000 (in person only)
- Year 6 $80,000 (started online)
- Year 7: $80,000-$150,000 (In person and online)
- Year 8: $150,000-$350,000 (In person and online)
- Year 9: $350,000-$600,000 (In person and online)
- Year 10: $600,000-$1,200,000 (In person and online)
- Year 11: $1,200,000-$1,500,000 (In person and online)

Before moving things online I built my coaching business purely in person over the span of my first 5 years from $0 — $80,000.

I was happy with that! But I was stuck…I plateaued

Years 6-10 when we shifted to building our online audience and brand you can see the big jump in the revenue.

So what took me 11 years to build to $1,500,000 per year coaching business I think I could do in less than half the time knowing what I know now.

That's what I want to share with you. To save you time and energy and prevent you from making a bunch of the mistakes I made along the way.

But before we get to that let me tell you about who I am and how we got here.

Contents

CHAPTER 1

My Story

Sometimes I hear stories about these GREAT coaches who tell their stories and say they KNEW they wanted to be a coach from a young age—like it was always in their blood.

That wasn't the case for me. I really stumbled upon coaching by accident.

I grew up in a small town in Pennsylvania in the 90s and early 2000s, and just like a lot of boys my age, we focused most of our time outside playing with friends and being obsessed with sports.

I played all different sports growing up and found I was naturally pretty good at most of them. I could never run fast nor jump high, but I always excelled in any eye-hand coordination-based activities—baseball, basketball, throwing footballs, ping pong, darts, etc. Activities based primarily on eye-hand coordination and not having to run fast or jump high, and I did pretty well.

I spent most of my time from age 6 to 13 playing baseball and basketball anytime I had the chance. School and sports, that's really all I cared about.

I can remember going to school from 7 to 3 and then rushing home to play sports with my friends—either organized practices or just to play pick-up at the local park.

Sports were a lifestyle for us. It was 24/7.

So naturally, since that was all we were focused on, we all dreamed of being professional athletes. We all thought for sure we would be on TV one day playing sports—baseball, basketball, football—you name it.

We were all from such a small town and never really got out of our bubble. So, if you were a decent athlete locally, you really didn't have any idea that there were literally millions of other kids across the country just as good or better.

We didn't know that, and that was good. It enabled us to dream.

Well, fast forward a few years, and you start to travel a bit and see those other kids and see WOAH… these other kids from areas still within our own state are GOOD! Much better than us.

So that dream of playing on TV starts to fade pretty quickly, and reality starts to sink in. By about middle school age, I had a pretty good sense that I was never going to be the professional baseball or basketball player that I had hoped.

I had golfed maybe 2-3 times prior to this with my dad, who was an avid golfer. I'd just be out there hitting it around and honestly usually just being unbelievably frustrated at not being good at it right away. I remember those first few rounds being MUCH MORE FRUSTRATING than they were fun.

I'll never forget the first time I hit a golf ball. My parents had bought me a starter set of clubs to mess around with by a brand called "Ray Cook". It was a putter, 9-iron, 7-iron, 5-iron, and a driver. Some of you may have had a similar starter set.

He handed me that 9-iron one day in our backyard. We had about an acre behind our house but when I was younger it seemed like a mile.

He plopped down a ball and told me to give it a try.

I didn't really know how to hold the club correctly or how to stand next to it. But I was an athlete, I thought, so I just stood up next to the ball and made a swing.

To this day, it was one of the most solid golf shots I can remember ever hitting.

It was so flush! It was one of those golf shots that is so good that when you hit it, you almost feel nothing—just like cutting through butter.

"This is easy," I thought.

I liked that first shot so much that I thought I'd hit another. I proceeded to top, shank, or duff every other shot that day. I literally didn't hit a single good shot after that first one. HA!

This was the first time that I was really caught by the golf bug. If you golf at all, you know that feeling. You can hit 100 bad shots in a row, but it's that ONE GREAT shot you hit that hooks you and keeps you coming back. It was endlessly frustrating and exhilarating at the same time.

After that day, it was game on for me. I started to go all in on playing golf.

I started watching golf on TV all the time.

I quit playing baseball and basketball.

I was 13 at the time and just finishing middle school, and instead of my dreams of playing baseball or basketball professionally on TV, my focus now shifted to being one of those pros playing golf on TV.

Now, luckily for me, this same time frame when I was 13–14 years old was right around 2000–2002 when Tiger Woods had fully hit the scene and "Tiger-mania" was in full swing.

I look back on that and am incredibly thankful for the timing of that.

I JUST happened to get into and obsess with golf at the EXACT timing that Tiger Woods would come into the golf world and explode golf's popularity. He was a PERFECT role model and someone to look up to in terms of what he was able to do on the golf course for a young boy like me and millions of others around the globe.

He was doing things on the course people had never seen before—arguably the greatest golfer of all time—certainly the greatest period of golf from any one player during those years. So, I was double hooked!

But I still had the problem of not being that good yet.

Remember, I hit that first ball well, and then hit bad shot after bad shot after bad shot.

Well, I started to get better bit by bit over the coming years.

My dad and his friends always played every Saturday and Sunday at a local golf course (Bethlehem Municipal). Not only did I want to golf now and get better at the game, but it was also a great opportunity to hang out with my dad and his friends. Like many young boys, I think we look up to our fathers like they are our heroes; we admire them and want to be like them.

My dad, like all of the rest of us, certainly had his faults, but I still looked up to him and wanted to be like him. So, I started to play with them on the weekends and practice more on my own during the week after school and during the summers.

My dad and his friends were still much better than me.

I was used to being GOOD at sports—usually the BEST in my group of peers—and WINNING. Our baseball and basketball teams ALWAYS won the championship. We went undefeated for a period of YEARS in a row. I never lost a single game in any sport for 2 whole years.

Now, all of a sudden, I was getting beat every single weekend! I didn't love that.

But looking back on it, that made me MORE OBSESSED—hating to lose more than loving to win.

Sure, I wanted to get better for myself, but I REALLY didn't want to keep losing to my dad and his friends.

So, I would practice, practice, practice as much as I could.

We didn't have any money growing up, so I was never a member at a country club or any course. But I'll never forget that Christmas when I was 13–14 and first getting obsessed; my parents bought me a "season pass" to a local golf course.

It was the best gift I could have ever imagined! Exactly what I wanted!!

I never really wanted or liked material things growing up, but THIS—something I could USE—something I NEEDED—I knew would be a game changer.

This season pass meant that I could play as much golf as I wanted at this course (Southmoore Golf Course) during the week and after 3 p.m. on weekends. I could also hit a bucket of balls per day. This was all covered by the $400 season pass (remember this was in the early 2000s)

Southmoore Golf Course was about 15 minutes north of my house, so whenever I could get my mom or dad to take me, I would head up there and practice.

The next year, when I was 15, I found out I could get a job at the course picking balls. I could get paid to work and get my golf covered for free! This meant I could start to save some money and save my parents the $400 annual fee.

While the $5 per hour didn't make me a rich 15-year-old, money was always tight at the house, and I knew the $400 savings would be big for my parents. So I was in!

Once I was 16 and could drive myself to and from the course, my game REALLY got a lot better.

I got a job at a new course, Bethlehem Municipal—that same course my dad and his friends played at.

I would still pick balls on the range and work odd jobs around the course in exchange for minimum wage and free golf!

It was beautiful.

By the time I was 16, I was playing and practicing just about every day in-season and was able to get down to a "scratch" handicap. I was now shooting around par and beating my dad and all his friends on the weekend. This made me much happier than those earlier years of losing.

I was playing some local competitive golf and starting to win some tournaments— all local stuff, nothing major, but successes nonetheless. The playing pro dream was still intact.

I was able to get good enough to earn a golf scholarship to Lehigh University, a small local Division 1 college.

It was during this first year of playing college golf that I had the same experience I had when I was younger with other sports. As soon as I was exposed to other athletes outside of my little local area and saw HOW GOOD they were, I quickly had reality set in again.

They were so much better than me.

I remember our first few tournaments, seeing guys from other smaller Division 1 schools who were miles better than me. Frankly, and this is coming from a confident 18-year-old kid, I felt I was never going to be that good, no matter what I did.

And these weren't kids from big schools like Miami, Arizona State, Stanford, Duke, etc.; so if these kids were so much better, how good were those kids?!

Now at this time, a few key things happened that shifted my mindset and plans.

First, my first year in school just happened to be 2008, when the financial crisis was occurring.

So kids who were recruiting me a few months earlier and graduating from Lehigh University (a highly ranked academic school) with an MBA, who all had $100,000 jobs lined up after they graduated...well, those same kids now couldn't find a job at all.

I had thought before this that, OK, if my golf plans don't pan out, I can study economics, graduate from Lehigh, and get a six-figure job, no problem.

All of a sudden, that was off the table.

So my MAIN plan of playing golf professionally on TV seemed like it was no longer possible. And now my BACKUP plan of working in business didn't seem so good either.

During the 2008 crisis, I had never experienced anything like that growing up.

I knew nothing about the economy, how the world worked, etc.

All that I saw was what was right in front of me and what I was hearing.

Based on the news I was watching (which I didn't know at the time was a terrible idea), they were saying the world was coming to an end.

I just knew those guys couldn't get jobs, and I didn't want to go to school for another 5-6 years and end up just like them.

So, after my first year of school, all this was happening — not going to play on TV, not going to get a job in business/finance. What would I do?

This led me to another day that changed the trajectory of my life forever.

It was a hot August summer day in Pennsylvania. I was still working at the Bethlehem Municipal golf course—cleaning carts, picking balls, working in the pro shop, you name it.

This day I was picking balls on the range.

Now, not only was it HOT outside—one of those hot, muggy, humid, disgusting summer days— but to make matters worse for me, our driving range that I was driving the range picker on was also not a perfectly flat piece of earth. It was very bumpy. So it wasn't exactly the FUNNEST ride when you're dripping sweat and people are hitting balls at you every 30 seconds.

I was picking up the range like normal and pulled the picker off to the side of the range to remove the golf balls to take them to be washed and reloaded for the next set of golfers. And just as I was done cursing under my breath and walking up to load the balls, I happened to walk by the golf pro who was there giving a golf lesson.

This guy (who I didn't know at the time would turn out to be one of my best friends and mentors) made an offhand comment about just making $50 to give that golf lesson.

Now, as I was at the range, I had seen him and an older gentleman there on the range that he was giving the lesson to.

I was out there on the range, bumping up and down, sweating my butt off, getting hit by balls every 30 seconds. He was there under a shaded area, laughing it up, and probably only hitting 10 balls or so over the whole 30-minute lesson.

They were mostly just talking and laughing, from what I could tell; it looked pretty easy.

Now, when he made this comment about the $50 for 30 minutes of work, I'm not saying I was the smartest kid in the world, but it didn't take me long to do some quick math in my head.

I was making about $7/hr at this point (yes, a big raise from my $5/hr two years earlier; you gotta start somewhere, right?). I did some quick calculations and thought to myself: $7 per hour; if I worked a full 8-hour shift, I would make $56; then, after I paid taxes on that, it worked out to be almost exactly that same $50.

So I needed to work a FULL eight hours, picking balls on that damn bumpy driving range, out in the heat, to make THE SAME $50 he just made in ONLY 30 MINUTES!

It wasn't hard to figure out I would rather be in the shade laughing it up for 30 minutes versus the 8 hours.

So now a few things were coming together at the same time:

1. I knew I wasn't going to be good enough to play pro.

2. I didn't want to go to school for 5-6 years and not get a job.

3. I'd rather make $50 in 30 minutes than 8 hours.

And THIS is how my coaching career started

I didn't come out of the womb thinking I wanted to be a coach.

I didn't have a passion for it.

It never even crossed my mind—not until I was put in a position where it seemed like the next logical thing to do. Part logic, part I needed money, part luck.

The very next day, I talked with Paul—the pro who was giving the lesson—and told him I was interested in learning to give golf lessons and if he could help me get started.

The very next week, I gave my first golf lesson.

Ten years later, I made my first $1,000,000 in a year coaching.

Crazy.

Let me show you how I did it.

FOCUS FIRST, AND ALWAYS, ON GETTING GREAT AT YOUR CRAFT

I knew that before I could focus on building my business, I needed to focus on getting better as a coach. My initial goal was to be the best golf coach in the world. I figured if I could do that, everything else would take care of itself.

I had that half right.

The MOST IMPORTANT thing we can do to build an incredible coaching business and the lifestyle that comes along with it is to ACTUALLY BE A GREAT COACH.

So whether you are just beginning your coaching journey, are somewhere in the middle of it, or you've been coaching for decades, at the top of the priority list needs to be getting better at our craft.

It's a process that never ends, something we all need to keep top of mind. Certainly, in the beginning years, this is MOST important.

The first part of being a great coach is understanding the actual mechanics of what you're talking about. For me, it was GOLF SWING MECHANICS. How the thing you're coaching works.

Whether you're a coach who focuses on a sport, fitness, finance, life, or you sell services like insurance, marketing, or any other industry where you sell coaching or services, knowing WHAT THE HELL you're talking about needs to be step 1.

That means studying and knowing your topic inside and out, industry trends, and everything going on in the world of your industry.

For my first 5 years, I was OBSESSED with getting better at coaching. Very similar to when I first learned to PLAY golf; in the beginning, I stunk. No one is any good when you first start something, and I certainly was not a good golfer when I started.

But over time and through lots and lots of practice, I became GREAT. Coaching was much the same for me. When I first started, in those beginning lessons, I stunk.

That's OK. That's INEVITABLE. NO ONE is good in the beginning. The only way to BECOME great is to get THROUGH that and do the coaching reps.

But doing the coaching reps itself isn't enough. You need to study OUTSIDE of the classroom, spending time with focused energy to get better at coaching outside of your coaching hours themselves.

Here's what I did to improve that you can too:

1.I read every book I could get my hands on related to golf and the golf swing.

I bought some, borrowed some from others, rented from local libraries—any way I could get my hands on the information to help me learn.

2. I watched every show, video, etc., on the topic.

I used to watch every golf teaching show on the golf channel NO MATTER what, watching them live or recording and watching later. Without exception, I did whatever I needed to do to watch everything. I wanted to know what those other pros knew.

Now with YouTube videos and social media, there are a lot more opportunities to easily find content from the top people in your space to watch and learn from them.

3. I shadowed other coaches (at my club first) and then gradually in my local area, eventually expanding out throughout the state.

Most coaches are happy to allow you to shadow and LIKE the fact that you think highly enough of them to want to do that. Especially if you're a hungry younger coach and they can sense and feel your aspirations to improve. You learn A LOT from shadowing and seeing what other coaches do, especially the "good ones."

Not only can you learn from this what you SHOULD DO, but you will also see some areas and things they do that you can improve upon. You learn a lot about the actual mechanics of your coaching, but you also learn about how to structure a lesson, how to interact with people, how to start a lesson, close a lesson, and all of the other ancillary aspects of coaching.

4. I got a lot of actual coaching reps.

Of course, at the end of the day, there is no replacement for actual coaching reps—getting thrown into the fire and learning HOW TO DO the thing by actually DOING THE THING.

This should be a main focus in the early years.

Think to yourself: how many hours do I think I would need to coach to reach a world-class level where it would be undeniable?

Maybe 10,000 hours?

Divide the amount you think by your first 5–10 years of coaching, and that will give you a good idea of how many reps you will need to get there.

5. I recorded my coaching sessions to review later.

This is another one that helped me a lot. I heard about another coach in a different industry recording their coaching sessions and watching them back, and I thought that was genius.

I would record some of my early lessons and watch them back to see what I could do differently.

Just as a heads up: if you haven't seen or heard yourself on video, don't be surprised if you're thrown off by how you actually look and sound. That's normal; you'll get better over time.

But it's an awesome source of FEEDBACK, and the video never lies.

Just like if you want to lose weight, stepping on a scale never lies and tells you like it is—for better or worse.

Filming our coaching sessions and watching them back serves much the same purpose.

This could be filming your coaching sessions if you're a coach or you delivering your service/sales process if you're delivering services.

Watching back YOU doing what YOU are doing/selling.

Then, if you are feeling really bold and ambitious (and can find other coaches to help), send these videos to other people and get feedback from them.

I did this early on in some of the Facebook Golf Coaching groups I was involved with, and it helped me a ton.

I would suggest filming at least ONE of your coaching sessions per week to review for your first 2 years.

Less than 1% of all coaches will actually do this. If you do, this will make you better than 99% of your coaching competition with this one habit alone.

6. I got involved with groups or networks of like-minded coaches.

I had this with several online groups, primarily Facebook groups in those early days, where we could have daily discussions on coaching topics to help each other.

I learned so much in those early years from those other coaches in those groups that helped me improve my coaching.

This could be an online group you find or a group of your peers in person.

Find like-minded people in your industry to have daily/weekly discussions with. We learn, grow, and improve MUCH faster when we work together versus alone.

7. I went to coaching events and seminars.

This was another big one for me that helped a lot—not just for the information that I would learn while I was at these events, but also from the PEOPLE you meet. I made so many lifelong connections from those early seminars I attended.

The info is great, but it's often the conversations afterward or in the hallways on breaks that are the real game changers!

One of my mentors from afar, Patrick Bet-David, says that he has made it a habit to go to a business seminar once per quarter (4 per year) for the past 10 years.

Imagine if you did that. Would you be better or worse off 10 years from now? By how much?

You could LEARN something or MEET SOMEONE who could change your life forever from just ONE of these events.

8. I worked under a great coach.

I was fortunate to have a few great pros at my course that took me under their wing.

Being able to watch them coach, ask them questions, and bounce ideas off of them was all invaluable in those early years.

I also went outside of my club and found someone about an hour and a half from me—a coach named Dom Dijulia who was one of the top-ranked coaches not just in my state, but in the entire country.

I worked for him for a summer so I could learn more, watch him teach, and help assist with some of his summer camps and clinics.

I learned so much from just being around him—how he taught, how he ran his business, and just being involved in the day-to-day operations.

Guess how I got that job?

I reached out to him via email, introduced myself, and asked if I could come shadow him for the day.

He said yes, let me watch him coach for a few hours, and then took me out to lunch.

It was AWESOME!

It was that OUTREACH and going to SHADOW him that created that OPPORTUNITY.

Of course, this isn't an all-inclusive list of things to do to improve your coaching, but these 8 strategies helped me a ton and will help you as well.

Let's talk next about growing and optimizing your in-person coaching business before we get into the online strategies.

CHAPTER 2

How To Start And Grow Your In-Person Coaching First

So, as I was using the 8 strategies above to help me LEARN to BECOME a better coach, I still had to do some things to actually build my coaching business and make some more money.

Remember earlier when I said:

"I knew before I could focus on building my business up, I needed to focus on getting better as a coach. My initial goal was to be the best golf coach in the world. I figured if I could do that, everything else would take care of itself.

I had that half right

The part about intentionally getting better as a coach and trying to be the best in the world was good.

The part that I didn't get right is the "everything would take care of itself."

Of course, as we get better at coaching, what does that mean?

It means that we get a lot of natural benefits:

1. Our students will get better and better results.

2. Those better results increase the odds of them staying with us longer and paying us more money over time.

3. Those better results also increase the odds of them telling other people they know about us, gaining us business from word of mouth.

All of that helps.

But that doesn't build you a $1,000,000 coaching business overnight.

It helps you grow; it makes you more money; but we need to stack other things on top of that.

That was the part I didn't have right with that thought.

Everything wouldn't take care of itself; I—me—needed to MAKE IT HAPPEN.

Of course, it needs to be based on the foundation of you getting your students great results. Actually being good at coaching; actually improving your students or your services working.

But when you have ZERO students to start, what do you do?

Or if you already have students/customers but aren't growing like you want.

Remember my coaching revenue increase per year from earlier:

- Year 1: $0-$7,500 (in person only)
- Year 2: $7,500-$15,000 (in person only)
- Year 3: $15,000-$30,000 (in person only)
- Year 4: $30,000-$60,000 (in person only)
- Year 5: $60,000-$80,000 (in person only)
- Year 6: $80,000 (started online)
- Year 7: $80,000-$150,000 (in person and online)
- Year 8: $150,000-$350,000 (in person and online)
- Year 9: $350,000-$600,000 (in person and online)
- Year 10: $600,000-$1,200,000 (in person and online)

Here's what I did to grow from $0-$80,000 before we went online:

1. Worked with that golf pro Paul for him to send me students and split the fee.

How I got my VERY first lessons was from that golf pro I told you about that I saw on the range that day.

I talked with him about wanting to teach, and he agreed to allow me to do it and help me learn. What a blessing that was.

It just so happened that at that same time, when I was picking balls that day and heard him say that $50 comment that led me to want to coach, well, he was just starting to get to the point where his coaching schedule was getting too full!

He was getting more people coming in asking for lessons than he could handle.

Lucky timing for me!

So we talked through this a bit and made an agreement that he would send me a few students to start (1-2 per week) that were more beginner players that I could work with.

This would be good for me since the students were beginners; they didn't know much yet, and so I felt like I would actually be able to help them.

I shadowed Paul and another golf teaching professional while they coached students a few hours per week. I watched about 20 or so lessons from start to finish before I gave my first lesson.

I felt like this gave me a good enough base to understand how the process worked, how they helped their students, and a little bit of actual coaching knowledge.

The agreement was that we would charge them the $60 lesson fee that he was charging and split the money 50/50.

$30 for him and $30 for me.

He would give me the students, and I would coach them. Win-win!

Overnight, I went from making $7/hour to $30/hour. That was a nice raise.

Of course, I was only doing 1-2 lessons per week to start, but still! $30 per hour—I thought I was rich!

If you're starting from scratch or stuck at your current level, this is a great avenue to explore.

Who else do you know in your industry that may be full or close to full that you could help coach their clients and split the revenues with them?

Even in the beginning, if you need to fill your book, make the split more enticing for them—50/50, 60/40, 70/30. It's not about the money for you yet; it's about getting the opportunity to get the coaching reps and build your student base.

2. I made up for a lack of skill in the beginning with EFFORT and CARE.

Now, in the beginning of coaching (and you know this yourself if you've been through it), we all stink.

Like I said earlier, those first set of lessons—probably the entire first year—I was no good.

But we have to get through that process.

Did I help some of these golfers get better?

Maybe.

Some got better, some stayed the same, and some got worse.

A far cry from my coaching now, where my expectation is a 100% improvement rate.

Did I give them way too much information?

Absolutely.

A lot of us, in the beginning of coaching or delivering services (I think subconsciously because of our lack of knowledge), try to overcompensate for that by giving our students too much to do—too much information.

It's sort of a "look at me, look how much I know; see, I know what I'm doing."

We are trying to convince ourselves as much as them, really.

But did I make up for those lack of early results with effort—with really caring about the student and how they were doing?

Of course.

In the beginning, we make up for our lack of skill with effort and showing we care.

Of course, our students are there to improve whatever they are there for, but lots of them will stay with us if we show we care and are willing to go above and beyond to help them.

I would follow up with them in the beginning to check in a lot, see how they were doing, and if they had any questions — offer additional help for free, etc. Whatever I needed to do.

I knew I could keep them coming back if I genuinely was doing everything I could do to help.

How do you show you care?

By actually caring — a lot.

Between #1 and #2, that got me through my first year of coaching and about $7,500 of revenue.

It was a start!

3. DELIVER on your current set of students and get them to stay.

A principle that is very important to understand when it comes to growing your business is the lifetime value of your customer. That means how much each of your customers will pay you over the life of them being your customer.

We'll dig into this more later when we get into the online pieces, but understanding that it's always easier and better to get more from your current customers than to get a new customer.

This was a big part of my revenue going from $7,500 to $15,000 in year two and $15,000 to $30,000 in year three.

At this point, I was still only teaching a few hours per week while working other jobs at the course as my "full-time" job.

I had been promoted from picking the range to working inside the pro shop and cleaning golf carts. Still, roughly the same $7/hour pay but better work conditions.

No longer did I have the bumpy range and people hitting balls at me to deal with; now I was inside the air conditioning behind the cash register.

Dealing with all the customers coming in each day was better than picking the range (only by a little.)

This was a valuable thing for me to learn as I was heading toward working in the golf industry as my career. I was into the teaching, but there was still a chance I would get a traditional golf pro job.

Work in the pro shop some, run some tournaments, teach some—I had seen other people at seminars and things I was going to who did this and seemed to like it.

I quickly realized during years 2-3 that that was not the path I wanted to take. I didn't hate it, but I didn't enjoy it as much as coaching, nor did I think the potential was the same as what I could do teaching full time.

So, I slowly went from teaching those 1-2 lessons per week to 3-5 per week to 10-15 per week over those first 3 years.

I'll talk more later about how I did that, but the core of that was keeping around those first customers who came in.

Every current customer I had that stayed meant one less spot I needed to fill the next week.

During this time, I also started to get my own customers versus Paul giving them to me, which meant I could keep 100% of the lesson fees—minus 10% to the golf course.

I was able to raise my personal hourly rate from $30/hr to $40/hr to $60/hr.

So, after my first 3 years of coaching part-time, I was able to:

1. Spend most all of my energy getting better at coaching by studying and shadowing other coaches.

2. Learn to coach better by getting in a bunch of reps.

3. Increase my coaching revenue from $0 to $30,000.

4. This was all while I was still working at the golf course 20-30 hours per week and realizing that that was not the path I wanted to take.

5. Get word-of-mouth from the first/current set of students.

Part of delivering on that first set of clients was to get them to stay with me for longer periods of time. This allowed me to fill one of my spots for the next week without having to get someone new in there.

But what about the other spots?

How would I fill those other spots every week?

This is where word-of-mouth from those initial students played a big role.

Even though in year 1 (and maybe some of years 2-3), as I was first learning to coach, my coaching itself, in terms of the results they were getting, was not great—it was okay, but nothing to write home about.

I made sure I took great care of them. I cared a lot and went the extra mile, like I explained previously.

Now, the benefit of that (outside of me wanting to genuinely help them) started to show up in my business from them telling their other friends or anyone who ever asked about golf lessons about me.

I knew if they liked me, saw how much I tried to help them, and that I would do whatever I could to help them, that they would always remember that.

And when they were ever presented with the opportunity to tell someone they knew, or if anyone ever mentioned golf lessons, they would think of me.

I started to see the effect of this right away.

At the end of lessons, or in the following days/weeks/months, I would start to get messages from them saying, "Hey Eric, my friend _____ is interested in lessons as well. Can I send them your number?"

Then the person they knew would come in, and I would follow the same process. I would take great care of them so they would also stay, and they would also tell other people.

You can see how this would start to compound over time.

Slowly but surely, I was filling my lesson book.

Since I was still working at the course 20-30 hours per week and trying to spend as much time as I could studying coaching and shadowing others, I could only coach a certain number of hours per week.

At this point, I could only really handle up to 20 hours per week and was at $30,000 in revenue—already more than double what I was making in 20-30 hours in the shop.

I had a decision to make: could/should I just start coaching full time and not work at the course anymore?

I was already filling most of my coaching spots; I was starting to get better at actually coaching and helping people. Could I continue to build on it?

I decided I was ready to do that, and Paul and the course were nice enough to let me try. No need to work in the shop anymore; it was time to coach full time.

And that's exactly what I did next.

I was able to coach full time in year 4 and take my revenue from $30,000 to $60,000.

And then from $60,000 to $80,000 in year 5—my final year of in-person-only coaching before we took things online.

From $7/hr part-time to $80,000 in 5 years. So cool to look back on.

The next few strategies on the list really helped to create this doubling in revenue within the next year and get me to that final $80,000 mark.

5. Ask for referrals from the first/current set of students.

I had my current set of students staying for longer and longer periods of time.

That was awesome; it helped fill a lot of my spots.

They were kind enough to tell other people they knew who were interested in golf lessons about me. That word of mouth led to new students. Those new students, I would also work my hardest to get them to stay. That helped fill more spots.

These new students (word of mouth from my first set) would also tell other people; they would then come in, and the cycle would continue.

This was great; I was getting some great momentum, but I was still only filling up 15-20 lessons per week at this time.

I was able to raise my rates to $80 per hour at this point. We'll dig more into increasing rates and supply and demand later.

So it was nice—I was making more money—but I was also spending it all at the time just as fast as it was coming in.

In fact, in those early years, I was a lot less disciplined with my newfound money and got myself into about $50,000 worth of debt.

I bought a new car, I bought a Trackman launch monitor, and I was spending more money each month than I was earning. I was young, dumb, and having fun.

So I needed to make more just to cover my expenses.

I needed to fill more lesson spots to do this. I had just increased my rates to $80 to help, so I didn't feel like I could charge any more, nor did I have the demand to justify it; so the only thing I could think of was to fill more coaching spots.

Instead of 20 per week, I wanted to do 30+ coaching hours per week.

I figured that amount, with our 8-month or so long golf season, would be enough to cover my yearly expenses.

This led me to the next few small tweaks I added to help fill those additional spots I now had available.

I saw that the word of mouth was great, but that only happened if THEY took the time to MAKE THAT HAPPEN. If someone happened to ask them about golf and they HAPPENED to think of me.

I thought I should try and take control of that process myself, and instead of HOPING they told someone about me, what if I took it upon myself to ASK THEM if they knew someone who they could recommend?

This is when I learned about the power of REFERRALS.

At the end of every lesson for a new student, I would say something like:

"Hey _____, thanks for coming out today! I really enjoyed today's lesson and I'm confident we are going to see great results with your game! Do you happen to know anyone else who may be interested in improving their golf game as well? I would love to be the one to help them!" Something simple like that.

I was AMAZED at the results this led to. I would say AT LEAST 75% of these people would say, "YES, as a matter of fact I do know someone _____ who's been talking about getting lessons."

Now this wouldn't ALWAYS lead to me actually getting a new student, but it OFTEN led to me getting the contact info for this new potential customer and getting them in my orbit.

Even if they didn't come in for a lesson right away, they were now aware of me if they ever did want to get a lesson, and I had their contact info to follow up with them.

I would ask my student to introduce me to their friend via text or email, and they were always happy to.

I filled a bunch of my new spots with this small tweak.

Taking the initiative to ASK them for a referral instead of just waiting for the natural word of mouth to happen (which would still happen anyway).

6. Using FREE to fill open spots

Now I was really rolling. I was utilizing all of the above strategies to help me fill more and more of my coaching spots.

I was out of the pro shop and able to coach full-time.

I realized about this same time that I DID NOT like living in debt and spending more than I was making; so I made some lifestyle changes.

I sold my car, reduced a bunch of expenses, and got completely out of debt within about 12 months.

Now I was MAKING MORE, SPENDING less, and could actually start to SAVE some money!

Up until this point in my life, I never had more than about $1,000 in savings to my name. For the first time over winter, I was able to save $10,000.

Another point I'll never forget is where I felt rich. That $7/hr to $30 jump felt AMAZING, and saving $10,000 was a big moment for me. Around this same time I discovered another game changer for my business—something that would also later prove really important for our online offers but helped finish off those last 2 years of growth in year 4-5 when I was coaching full-time.

Offering a FREE lesson. I've found time and time again the BEST way to get new customers through your door to TRY your coaching or service is FREE. ESPECIALLY in the beginning years and when you are not nearly as full as you would like. If you don't have enough DEMAND of customers coming in to fill your spots and raise your prices, you need to CREATE the DEMAND. You do that by making them an "irresistible offer" (more on this later).

Make them an offer so good they feel stupid saying no. An offer so good that they HAVE TO try it. What's better and easier than free? You want to get better at golf and are thinking of taking lessons? How about I give you a lesson FOR FREE. No strings attached, no risk. Just a FREE lesson. They have nothing to lose and everything to gain.

I don't remember exactly WHERE I saw it, but I saw another coach offering a FREE SWING EVALUATION in one of those online Facebook groups I mentioned (see the value of those earlier improvement strategies come in many forms). I thought it was a really good idea, and he was explaining how he was getting great results from it.

So I decided to give it a try. The golf course was nice enough to allow me to send out an email to their email list. I wrote something along the lines of:

"FREE LESSONS AVAILABLE THIS SATURDAY 12-5

IF YOU WANT TO IMPROVE YOUR GAME, I WOULD LOVE TO HELP

FREE LESSON

NO STRINGS ATTACHED

12-5 PM

FIRST 5 RESPONSES ARE IN

EMAIL ME BACK AT ERIC@BETHLEHEMGC.COM
TO RESERVE YOUR SPOT"

I wasn't sure what the response would be like, but by the end
of the first day, I had ALL 5 spots filled and a waiting list of
another 5-10 people who wanted in.

I was coaching my normal lessons during the week from 2-6
PM and Saturday mornings from 8-12, so I figured I could
add these in Saturday afternoons as needed. I had open time,
and most people were available on weekends. I didn't really
know what to expect nor how to handle these "free lessons"
as I had never done those before, but I was doing lots of
regular lessons, so I knew how to do that and figured I would
just run them the same way.

I had already built up the habit of asking my current students
for referrals, and that muscle I built with that habit helped a
TON during these free trials as I had to ask for the SALE at
the end. One of the things I saw from the other coach in that
online group was that he would do the free analysis, and then
AT THE END he would say something like:

"Hey student,

I hope you enjoyed today. We saw that by improving A, B,
and C, we would really be able to help you improve your
game. Obviously, in just one session we can't do it all, but

we got off to a great start improving A. IF you would like to improve B and C as well, I offer coaching that will help you do that.

Would you be interested in joining my _____ coaching plan so we can help you achieve _____ (goal) by _____ (date), like you mentioned you wanted to?"

He said he would convert 33-50% of these free analysis customers into PAID customers!

I went to the course that day and only had 1 lesson Saturday morning during my morning block, so I felt fresh and excited to do these lessons. I delivered the 5 lessons like normal, made sure I really listened to the student in the beginning to learn what their GOALS were, what they wanted to improve, and WHY they wanted to do it.

Not only would that help me guide the lesson, but I knew that would help me reiterate that during the close and asking for the sale.

I gave them my normal lesson.

- Find out what they want to improve and why
- Diagnose the current issues keeping them where they are and holding them back from achieving those goals
- Explain those root issues

- Start to work with the student on improving those root issues
- Explain what they need to do on their own to continue this improvement
- Take notes and wrap up

Then I would ask for the sale.

To my amazement, I got 3 out of the 5 people to buy into my PAID COACHING plans.

I did the same thing during the next 4 Saturdays and got exactly 10 out of 20 students to buy into my coaching.

That was 10 new spots filled.

10 new chances to keep these students long term.

10 new chances to get customers from their word of mouth.

10 new chances to get new customers from asking them for referrals.

Another compounding snowball effect on my business—a SMALL THING that leads to HUGE results.

If you are just starting or have coaching spots you want to fill, I would HIGHLY ENCOURAGE you to consider offering a FREE coaching session to help fill those spots.

You will sacrifice SOME TIME, but you will get GREAT RESULTS.

7. Shifting from ONE hour/one-off pricing to monthly/packages

During the same time I was learning about and testing these free trials, I was also seeing something from a bunch of the more successful coaches about selling "coaching plans" vs. one-off lessons. I had never heard of a "coaching plan" before. Up until this point, I had only sold one-off lessons.

If my lesson fee was $80, I was just trying to get the person to come in and pay my one-hour fee. Then at the end of that lesson, I would try and book the next lesson—again for a one-time fee of $80.

This worked OK, but once I learned about PRE-SELLING coaching packages, it was another small tweak that led to much better and more PREDICTABLE revenue.

Basically, these coaching packages were selling multiple lessons at a time right away instead of only one at a time.

And I found out those same customers who were paying $80 as they went were more than willing to pay $320 at a time for a set of 4.

This was great; now I was getting $320 payments at a time vs. the $80.

I also knew for sure they were now coming for at least 4 more sessions, and I didn't have to worry about collecting payments at the end of every single session.

I realized that people are used to paying MONTHLY payments for just about everything else in their lives anyway.Mortgage, rent, car payments, insurance, etc.—most all are paid with ongoing monthly payments. People were used to it.

It made total sense to me.

I realized a bunch of other coaches in those online groups were already doing this—selling 3, 5, 10 lessons at a time—all paid up front.

I tried that and started to offer packs of 3, 5, and 10 and had good success.

But once I tried the ongoing monthly packages, that is when my revenue grew to a whole other level.

I created a new monthly program: $320 per month—one lesson per week—plus support in between (answering questions, ongoing feedback, etc.).

One of the coaches that I learned from said that when he was selling his packages, we had to remember we are selling MORE than just that one hour of coaching with us.

We are selling our coaching as a whole—the total package.

If they are sending you emails in between sessions with questions, if they are sending you swing videos to critique in between to make sure they are doing things correctly, or contacting you for advice, that all has to be part of the package.

This was the first time that I heard about the idea of offering pricing and services beyond just the hourly coaching.

Again, it made total sense to me.

So as I was getting people to sign up for the 3, 5, and 10-hour packages and then the $320 monthly, I started to feel brave and, instead of offering the $320 ($80 x 4 hours), I increased my rate to $399/month to include access to those other services in between the sessions.

And guess what?

The people loved it! No issues or pushback whatsoever.

I was a little bit nervous about offering 3, 5, and 10 hours at a time to people, but they loved it; they stayed longer, and I made more money.

Then I was nervous about the ongoing monthly plans.But the same thing happened; they liked it, stayed longer, and I made more money.

So, now I was making $399/month per student.

Not only did I make more money, but it was more predictable; I didn't have to worry about collecting money at the end of every lesson, I didn't have to worry about cancellations. I could bank on predictable monthly income for the first time in my coaching life.

I was growing and making more money the other way as well, but remembering to collect the money every time was something I always had to worry about in the back of my mind. Would they forget to bring payment? Would they cancel last minute? If they canceled before they paid, I made nothing.

Well, not anymore.

Monthly recurring payments for your clients is something, if you don't already use, I would highly recommend thinking about how you can implement.

You can offer a one-time free session/consultation, like I did, but then the sell from there into paid coaching isn't into another one-time session; it's into an ongoing program/service that makes sense for their goals.

And this is something you are establishing up front, like I mentioned in the free trial flow.

You make sure in the beginning of your consultation you ask questions to get clear on what their goals are and what they want to achieve.

Then you go through and diagnose what's holding them back and leading to their issues.

Then, what needs to be done to fix those.

When you and the student are both clear on what they want, what's holding them back, and what needs to be done to fix it, I've found most people from there are incredibly reasonable.

When you lay out the plan, it will be easy to see that you both need time to work together to get to their goals.

And you can offer a suggestion for which service/package they should go with.

Explaining that this is the best option for them to accomplish the goals they want to achieve (repeat these goals back to them during this process) and why this program will help them get there.

Not everyone will buy, but enough will, and they are very likely to be your best customers and the ones you get the best results with anyway.

They get that things take time; they like and trust you and are willing to invest to get those results.

Here's an example of how I would have presented this:

"Hey John,

Great session today! I love the progress we are making on _____. You're doing a great job! Based on your goals you mentioned of wanting to hit the ball more solid, lower your scores into the 80s, and beat your buddy Rick, I feel confident we can accomplish all of those within the next 4 months with my _____ coaching plan.

We saw, based on our analysis, we need to fix _____, _____, and _____. That's exactly what this plan is designed to do. It's $399/month and includes weekly lessons.

You're going to love the results we get!

Are you opposed to moving forward with the _____ plan?"

8. Raising Prices Based on Demand

As time went on using the above strategies, I was able to fill my available spots.

So if I was offering 20, 25, or 30 hours per week, I was getting all of those spots filled with my current students.

This was really my first big lesson on supply and demand.

I had studied this in school and understood the basic concept, but like many things in school, when you learn them, it takes doing them in the real world to fully comprehend things.

Supply and demand for us in the coaching or service-based world is relevant to what price we are able to charge.

When supply is set at a certain amount for us (how many hour spots you coach and are able to sell—e.g., 20 hours per week), our ability to raise (or have to lower) our price to fill those spots is dictated by demand.

Demand is how many people want those spots.

If you have 20 spots open and only 10 people want them, demand is lower than your supply, and you won't be able to raise your prices (and may need to lower them to fill your spots).

If you have 20 spots and 20 people (or close to it) to fill those, then your supply and demand are even. The same amount of spots you have open, you have people who want them.

But something really cool happens for us when our demand is above our supply.

That means if we have 20 spots open but 30, 40, 50 (or anything above 20) want those spots, then we can raise our prices.

Anytime demand is higher than supply, you can raise prices.

Anytime demand and supply are the same, the prices stay the same.

Anytime demand is less than your supply, prices come down (if you want to fill all the spots).

So the goal with all of the above strategies to grow your in-person business is all about increasing your demand and keeping your supply the same (how many hours you coach).

Controlling this is so important because it allows us to raise our prices over time.

This is especially important and a big reason why we want to grow our audience online (we'll get to that later).

So when I started with 1-2 lessons per week, then 5-10, then 10-20, and then about 30 lessons per week when I went full-time, I had to fill those extra spots with free trials, word of mouth, referrals, etc.

But once they are all full (and you keep using the above strategies), now all those referrals and word-of-mouth new customers who want in can't get in because you're full.

As you already know in your own life, we humans tend to want even more what we can't have. As a business, this allows us to raise prices.

You can start with raising prices on anyone new. That's what I did. So anyone who was in at $80 or the monthly prices was able to keep that price point, but anyone new would be at the new price (for me, that was $100). That would eventually go from $100 to $350/hour, but I ended up at $100 before we shifted things online.

So my current base of customers was able to stay in at $80/$399 per month, but as soon as one of those would leave, someone new would come in at $100/$499 per month, which was my new pricing model.

So slowly, the original people leave, new people come in, and you make more money without having to work more hours.

I found that once current students knew the prices had gone up for new clients, they wanted to stay even longer because they realized they were getting a deal and a discount based on the new prices, increasing their "lifetime value."

While I didn't know it at the time, increasing prices turned out to be a nice strategy to get current customers to stay longer and raise that lifetime value.

The other thing I realized over time is that as I raised prices and students needed to invest more and more money, they became better and better students.

The worst students I ever had were the ones that did things for free (and didn't convert) or got in on the lower price points.

The more someone would invest, the more serious they would take things (because they had to pay more).

They showed up to the sessions more prepared, they listened better, they did everything I said, and they would practice more in between sessions.-

They were more invested because they invested more.

Something for you to consider as you figure out your pricing model: the more people pay, the better the student they are.

Figure out how many hours you want to coach (supply) and control that; keep that constant. Work to increase your demand (how many people want those spots), and you will be able to increase your coaching rates. We'll discuss this more when we talk about growing your audience online, but here's what my lesson rate increases looked like. You'll see I've been able to raise my prices 12 times since I started:

- $30/hr — $40/hr
- $40/hr — $60/hr
- $60/hr — $80/hr
- $80/hr — $100/hr

- $100/hr — $120/hr
- $120/hr — $150/hr
- $150/hr — $180/hr
- $180/hr — $200/hr
- $200/hr — $250/hr
- $250/hr — $300/hr
- $300/hr — $350/hr
- $350/hr — $1,500/4 hours

From $120 for 4 hours to $1,500 for 4 hours, a 12.5x increase in my rates came from controlling my supply (how many spots I coached per week) and increasing my demand (how many people wanted those spots).

Of course, a lot of that came from our online growth. I'm going to show you how to do that shortly, but first, here are a couple of other strategies that helped improve my in-person coaching business that I want you to be aware of.

CHAPTER 3

Things That Also Helped Grow Or Optimize My Coaching Business That I Recommend

1. Online Scheduler

I originally handled my lessons manually via text and email, trying to schedule back and forth. It was an absolute mess.

If you don't use an online scheduler, please get one immediately. I use Squarespace for this. It's about $20/month and saves you a ton of headaches and inconveniences compared to doing it all yourself.

2. Time Blocking Lesson Times

In the beginning of coaching, you may need to be a bit less flexible here and do the sessions when the student can. But as soon as possible, get control of your schedule and make it work for you.

I started by doing lessons whenever they could. I might have a lesson at 10 AM and then nothing else until 3 PM, creating huge time gaps in between sessions.

This wasn't the end of the world for me in the beginning because I worked at the course and could do other tasks in between.

But if this isn't the case for you, I wouldn't recommend it. Logistically, it can be really tough, especially if you are driving to and from your location to coach.

I also found there is a serious cost to task switching— coaching, then doing something else, then back to coaching, then to something else again. This isn't efficient.

Once you're in coaching mode, I found it best to just stay in that mode for a period of time (3-4 hours at a time for me was perfect).

Once I got busier, I built up my book and was doing 2-6 PM Monday through Friday and 8-12 on Saturdays, as I mentioned.

It was still during the hours that students can and want to take lessons, and it was time-blocked: 4 hours at a time.

Lessons booked back-to-back with no time in between.

This worked best for me.

I could get to the course before my sessions started, prep, do the lessons, and leave. No wasted time in between. I stayed focused and in coaching mode the whole time.

This worked much better for me than being at the course for about 8 hours with only those same 4 hours of coaching, resulting in wasted time in between.

As time went on and I became busier and more in demand, I changed the schedule to the hours that I wanted rather than what I perceived worked for students. And you know what I found? If you're in demand enough, the student is willing to work with your schedule and meet you when you want.

So my schedule moved to 12-4—a bit earlier in the day than I liked—and Saturdays only from 10-12, as I reduced my coaching hours with my prices increased.

Gain control of your schedule!

3. Book the Next Lesson Before the End of the Current Lesson

A smaller strategy, but one that helped me a lot, especially before I had the online scheduler and the monthly/ongoing packages when I was offering one-offs, was ensuring I booked the next lesson with the student before they left.

This practice helped reduce no-shows and cancellations.

This also inherently made them stay longer because we automatically booked another session right away.

So, at the end of the lesson, I would say, "Okay, John, great session today. Let's put you in for next Thursday at 5 PM. Does that work for you?"

If that time doesn't work, offer them another time slot that does.

Do everything you can to book that next lesson right away.

Remember, earlier when I said I learned that "everything didn't just take care of itself?" This is another one of those examples.

Don't let them take the lead and count on them scheduling later. Life happens, people forget—don't let your business depend on that.

You make it happen.

This was huge for me during those first years to help double my revenue and get people to stay longer. If you're in a similar situation, I would love for you to adopt the same habit; it will grow your business and usually takes less than 60 seconds.

4. Taking Notes at the End of the Session vs. After

This one is more of a time saver, but I used to make this mistake, and I see a lot of other coaches doing it as well.

I used to give my lessons and then go home later on and write down notes to send to them.

Now, the actual act of taking the notes and sending them is great. It shows you care, like we discussed earlier, helps with the retention of the student, and I think it is an area of opportunity for you to separate yourself and stand out from other coaches.

Doing the simple things well.

The problem with how I used to do it is I would do it later on after the lessons when I was at home. So, especially when I had 4-5 lessons that day, you can see how this would add up—sometimes as much as an hour or more of extra work when I got home.

I don't want extra work; neither do you.

First, sending notes to your student or customer is a great idea—recapping your sessions and agreed-upon "to-dos" after. But doing them during your sessions, at the very end, before you are done, is the way to do it.

So, if I had an hour-long lesson planned with someone, I would always end the actual coaching 5-10 minutes early to spend those last few minutes reviewing what we discussed and taking notes.

You could do these notes a few different ways: (Pick one)

1. I would write them down for them.

2. I would ask them to recap and have them write it down themselves to take ownership.

3. I would record them giving the recap and send them that video right there on the spot.

4. I would have them record me doing the recap, and that way they have it right on their phone.

See what works best for you, but take notes/recap and do it during the session.

Sometimes it's hard to see if you're not doing it yourself, but a few of these key things at the end of the lesson helped me a ton with being efficient and keeping customers:

- Taking/sending their notes
- Booking the next lesson
- Asking about referrals

All of that before the end of the lesson—every time.

So if your sessions are 60 minutes, plan for 10 minutes at the end so you stop the actual coaching at the 50-minute mark and add this in.

5. Pay Before vs. After Lessons (Reduce No-Shows/Cancellations)

This is something that took me a few years to learn and implement. If I needed to start over now, I would change this immediately, so I want to make sure I mention it here as well.

Get your students/customers to pay for your coaching/service before, not after, your lessons. Pay at the time of sign-up.

In those early years, I lost a bunch of money from people canceling, no-showing, etc., that I didn't need to lose. Especially in the early years, when I really needed all that money, I lost out on a bunch of revenue.

Have them pay up front.

6. Testing Group Lessons vs. One-on-One

The math on this one is pretty simple when it comes to revenue.

When you only have one person paying you per hour, you only make as much as they pay you. But when you have multiple people paying you per hour—for that same hour—you can obviously increase your revenues quite a bit.

Example:

You give one person an individual lesson for an hour and charge them $80; you make $80 total.

You give five people a group lesson and charge them each $50; you make $250 total.

Same amount of time (1 hour) but more than 3X the amount of money.

This is something to consider depending on your industry and how you deliver coaching.

The more people you can coach at once and the higher the amount you can charge, the more you can make per hour of coaching.

For me, I've tested various forms of this:

- Group lessons
- Group practice sessions
- Multi-day golf schools
- One-day golf clinics

Is your coaching something you could deliver to multiple people at once?

Could you make it as effective (or close to) as one-on-one?

The less personal your coaching needs to be, the easier this is.

If you have a general outline or program that you run everyone through, the same things, that's much easier to deliver to multiple people at a time.

I have personally seen this work in many industries, including sports coaching, fitness coaching, business coaching, etc.

You can have your entire program be group coaching or offer a combination of both.

One of the things I used to do at this time was offer players a monthly package that included both individual and group sessions.

It was similar to that $399 package I mentioned earlier — just a variation of that package.

They would pay $399 per month and get 2 private individual lessons each month, but they would also get access to a weekly "practice" group that I would host.

Every Tuesday and Thursday, I opened up a "group practice" hour where anyone within those monthly programs could come and get coaching. We would have some group drills we would be doing, but it also allowed me to check on their individual progress in between sessions to make sure they stayed on track.

Most players loved this and took full advantage.

I actually found the group environment to help a lot with the students' learning.

People helped each other, learned from each other, and they were all going through similar experiences and pain points, so it added a nice element I hadn't planned on.

As you start to plan out your dream life we'll talk about a bit later in this book, and figure out what sort of revenue you need to make per coaching hour to hit your revenue goals, keep this option in mind as a way to drastically increase your revenue per session.

These six are a few things that will help you optimize your coaching.

One final thing before we talk about building and monetizing online:

Let's talk next about how to actually structure your coaching sessions to maximize your customers' results and your business's revenue.

CHAPTER 4

My 9-Step Perfect Lesson Structure

Let's cover one last thing before we talk about scaling online and the events that completely changed my life both on and off the course.

I've evolved this process over time since I started, but I've found these are the 9 critical steps during each lesson and a few notes on each topic.

I learned some of these from shadowing other coaches, took some from those online groups, and just learned through trial and error on my own.

I do them all without any thought at this point, but I would make a conscious effort to ensure you do these during your sessions until they become automatic.

1. Greeting

We only have ONE chance to make a first impression, and we want to make sure we make the RIGHT one.

Of course, we are there to help our customers get better and achieve their goals, but we also have a business to run. And first impressions affect the bottom line of your business.

We want to LOOK the part, ACT the part, and DEMONSTRATE the part.

I've seen a lot of coaches over the years MISS some of these simple things and the NEGATIVE effect it had on their businesses.

Think about when you first meet someone you are working with in any capacity: what qualities do they have that you like?

What about those you don't like?

You don't have to "fake it" or put on a show; be, act, and look the part.

A) Dress and show up appropriately.

What do the top people in your space look like?

How do they dress?

You want to demonstrate that you are a PRO. You want these customers to see you as the person who's going to help them.

We want to look sharp, groomed, and well-dressed.

Walk the walk.

You MIGHT NOT get a customer just BECAUSE you look nice and are dressed well, but you sure as hell WON'T LOSE any because of it either.

IF we want to be a top player in our profession and charge premium prices over time, this CAN ONLY HELP us.

B) Show up ON TIME.

If you have a session with someone, you want to be there EARLY—not on time, not arriving at the same time as your student. Early, prepared, and ready.

I would always get to my first lesson about an hour ahead of time (never ever less than 30 minutes).

Some people show up early, so I wanted to be sure I was there and READY before they got there.

If you have some extra time here, you can use that to do any admin work, return calls/messages, etc., as needed.

Never ever late. Never ever. No matter what.

Not much you can do worse to make a bad impression on your customer than showing up LATE to your session that YOU SCHEDULED!

C) Make them FEEL good.

This is a BIG one that helped me and often goes overlooked:

People remember how you make them FEEL more than anything else. They will remember this MORE than any technical information you give them during your lessons.

So, let's take advantage of this:

Make them feel GOOD.

- Be happy to see them.

- Smile.

- Say their name (people love to hear their names) and it shows you are prepared and know who's coming if it's their first time, or you REMEMBER and CARE about them if they are a returning student.

- Physical touch, like a hand on the shoulder when greeting them, where appropriate.

I would always make it a point to do those four things when someone first arrived.

Tell them it was great to see them, greet them with a smile and a touch, say their name, and let them know I was excited for their session.

You want to keep this in mind and keep implementing this throughout the lesson and at the end.

MAKE THEM FEEL GOOD

When you make them feel good, they will associate feeling good with you and taking lessons with you and are much more likely to come back again.

Remember, from a business perspective, our goal is to keep these current customers around for longer and longer periods of time.

If they feel good, they will stay.

If they feel shitty, they will not.

So, give them compliments, keep smiling, tell them they are doing great, and encourage them.

Never ever talk down, make fun of, or be standoffish with a student (if you want them to come back).

2. Questions/Goals/What They Want/Why (Where Are We At, Where Do We Want to Go, What's Holding Us Back)

Once we are past the greeting phase and welcome them in, we want to get to Step 2, which is the information-gathering part.

This will adapt a bit depending on where the customer is with you in their journey and whether they are just starting or have been a returning customer, but certain things remain the same.

The first and most important part here is we get clear on:

A) Where they currently are (what's holding them back, their perceived issues, what they want to fix).

B) Where they want to go (what are their goals, dream outcomes, and why they really want to do those things).

It's important to get this information not only to help guide your coaching and your plans, but it's really important, like we mentioned earlier, to be able to sell them on longer-term coaching plans to accomplish those goals.

If you never get this information, we can still always fix the problems in front of us, but it's easy to get off course and also never have that ammo for the long-term coaching sale at the end.

You will sell less, and your business will suffer.

It's also important to keep those big picture goals in mind as you go through the lesson, especially if you are doing multiple sessions over a period of time.

You have lots of students, and they have lives outside of your coaching; it's easy to forget or get off track.

Having clear goals and a direction you are headed will make it much easier to stay on track and stay the course if you ever get off track or during any periods of struggle for them, reminding them of the goals, where we are heading, and why.

Getting the why they want it is important so we can tap into their emotions along the process as well.

To motivate them along the way, to keep them on track, to keep them accountable, and to sell them the ongoing coaching that they need.

It's the emotion that drives them to buy; good to keep in mind.

Understanding these goals in terms of general coaching structure will also obviously help you in the analysis and prescription phases below.

When it's time to lay out a plan and agree on expectations, those goals are very relevant.

Will you actually be able to help them achieve it?

How long will it take?

What sort of work will it take to get there?

No goals = no plans.

3. Analysis/Diagnosis (What's Causing Current Issues, Root Causes, What's Holding Back)

Once we are clear on where they want to go, we need to get clear on where they are.

This is the diagnosis part—diagnosing what their current issues are that are holding them back and why they are experiencing those issues.

For me, with golf, this would be me watching them actually hit balls, recording those swings, and reviewing those videos with the student.

Going over what's going on, the top root issues that are holding them back, and showing them a model of the "good version" so they can clearly see the difference between them and the "errors" and the model and the "correct" versions.

Depending on your coaching or industry, this could be you watching them perform to diagnose, asking more questions, reviewing their material, etc.

The objective here is for both you and them to be clear on the root issues that are causing the current problems holding them back.

4. Prescription/Plan of Solutions

Once you are both clear on those root issues, it's time for you to explain and show the solutions.

How will we fix the issues?

I would do this by:

- First, showing them the "correct" via video with the model, as I mentioned above.
- Physically showing them what they are doing wrong and how to do it correctly.
- Verbally explaining it to them as well.
- Getting them to explain it back to me in their own words so I know they understand.
- Having them write it down in their own words.
- Helping them start working on the solutions.

At this phase, you want to make sure both you and the customer are clear not only on what the issues are but also on how you are going to solve them.

I would say something like:

"Okay, John, we can see that your first issue was _____(problem #1), which was leading to _____(bad result), and the second problem was _____ (problem #2), which caused _____(bad result).

We are going to first focus on improving _____(problem #1) so we can fix _____(bad result) by doing _____(the drill, fix, solution). Make sense?

Okay, let's get started."

5. Execute on Plan/Start Working Through Solutions

For us in the golf world, this would usually come in the form of a physical drill.

Them swinging the club a certain way and either me physically moving them and guiding them through the good vs. bad motions

OR

Creating a practice station for them to use.

Either way, at this phase, we need to give them feedback on every rep.

Did they do it correctly or not? Why, and how to correct it?

For golf, we would use video feedback on every rep. I found this to work best for a few reasons:

- They were able to see themselves actually do the rep and didn't have to take my word for it.

- It's powerful to see on video what they actually did vs. what they felt like.

- Video never lies; like stepping on the scale, it is what it is—no opinion.

- Get them in the habit of using video so they would know how to do this on their own as well in between sessions.

In this beginning phase of actually working on improving something with the student, it's important to:

A) Only do 1-2 things at a time—less is more. Error on one.

B) Go slow (no one learns something at a fast speed first).

C) Do 1-2 rehearsals of the "correct" then try it, then 1-2 rehearsals again, then try again. I like 2 practice rehearsals, then 1 real rep.

D) Feedback on every rep.

Eventually, throughout the coaching session, you land on the best ways for them to improve; this is your plan.

The plan consists of:

- What are we doing? (The action)
- How are we doing it?
- How many reps?
- For how long?
- How do we know if we did it right or not?
- What defines success for us?

6. Make Sure They Know How to Execute on Their Own and Expectations from Now to Next Session

This phase is important to ensure success beyond just the time you spent together. To me, an effective session isn't really based on the progress you make during the session; it's based on the progress you make after the session—the time between your session and your next session.

That's what really dictates success or not.

Did they understand clearly what's going on, why, and how to fix it?

Did they do the work afterward to make the improvements?

Were they excited enough and bought in enough on the plan to work through any struggles?

So, in order to make sure we make that progress after the session before the next time I would see them, I added in this step to make sure they could explain back to me clearly the following six things:

1. What their main issues are that we are working on

2. Why these issues are happening

3. How we are fixing them

4. The expectations between now and X period in the future (next session)

5. The practice plan, the feedback, and how they know if they are doing it correctly or not

6. How much time they would spend per day/week/month

Leave no room for misinterpretation.

Same theme as earlier—don't hope and let it happen; make it happen. You control this as the coach/service provider.

7. Notes/Review

This would generally happen along with step 6, but when you're working through those details mentioned above in #6, you would be recording this or writing this down, and that would serve as your notes.

8. Schedule/Confirm Next Session

For ease of scheduling (even with an online scheduler), either you and them should book their next lesson time right then and there before they leave.

Ideally, over time you have people booked in coaching plans or monthly packages so they are already booked in multiple sessions. If that's the case, you are confirming the next session instead of booking it.

In the beginning phases of building your business, this is a big part of increasing the lifetime value of the customer and getting your current customers to stay longer, allowing you to make more money per customer versus having to find a new one.

9. Referral

After you have gone through the above steps and delivered your coaching, you have notes taken, and your next session is booked; the last step is to ask for the referral.

Something simple like the referral script from earlier works here:

"Hey _____, thanks again for coming in today. I really enjoyed today's lesson, and I'm confident we are going to see great results with your game! I'm looking forward to our next session on _____. Also, I was wondering if you happened to know anyone else who may be interested in improving their game as well? I would love to be the one to help them!"

This is a good one to use for new students on your first session or early in the process, but also with existing, recurring students.

With students you have already seen and already asked this to, it's okay to ask again after a period of time.

I would usually wait between 1-3 months after the first time I asked.

If they originally did not know anyone, I would say something similar to the above script but ask if they had thought of anyone or heard of anyone who's interested since that time.

If they originally did send me someone, I would thank them again for sending them over, tell them I'm really enjoying helping their friend with their game, and, of course, if anyone else comes to mind, please send them my way.

There's a fine line here—you don't want to be pushy, but you also don't want to leave things to chance. Don't be afraid to ask for continuing referrals!

That's my 9-step perfect lesson structure. You are likely already doing all or some of these. Take what you like and leave the rest, but these are the 9 steps I have always come back to in order to structure a great lesson and increase my coaching revenues!

CHAPTER 5

Getting Started Online

As I was learning and implementing all of the strategies and tactics that I mentioned above, I was succeeding in doing what I wanted to do: Grow my in-person business.

My mindset at the time never really went beyond that. I was just focused on the here and now and how I could grow my coaching business as much as possible.

Well, it worked.

In fact, it worked so well that by the time I was in my mid-twenties, I felt burnt out.

A few things happened to me all at the same time at this point in my life that led to the next big jump in both my business and my life.

First, I was feeling burnt out, like I mentioned.

All the tactics above worked! They worked so well that not only did I fill all my coaching hours, but I was filling even more than I wanted to.

I was working more than I wanted to, taking on too many clients, and I was starting to enjoy the coaching less and less. I felt tired.

I remember distinctly one day out on the range, after a long day of lessons, thinking to myself: Man, could I keep doing this until I'm 50 or 60 years old?

No way, I thought.

If I was already feeling burnt out in my 20s, how would I be able to keep doing this for the next 30 to 40 years?

That was an eye-opening thought.

Second, during the same week that I came to this realization, one of my friends happened to text me a video.

The video was of a guy by the name of Tony Robbins. I had never heard of him at that time, but I watched the video, and it really didn't do anything for me. But just to the right of that video on the screen was a recommended video with a guy named Jim Rohn.

To this day, I don't know exactly what it was about that video or Jim, or where I was in the moment, but I must have been ready to hear it.

I absolutely loved it. Everything he said felt like it hit me right in the heart.

He spoke with such logic, such simplicity. To the point— simple concepts—but POWERFUL!

It was the first time I had heard of "personal development."

Jim talked about the importance of making YOU better.

Working harder on YOU than you do on your JOB.

This was a new concept for me; no one ever told me about personal development, but I was hooked right away.

I watched that video of Jim over and over, and as I was watching it, more and more people in that personal development space were getting recommended to me.

It was at that time that I got turned onto guys like Grant Cardone and Gary Vaynerchuk—more guys who completely changed my perspective and changed my life.

At this point in time (2015-2016), guys like Gary and Grant were really gaining popularity, talking about building online businesses. Sales, online businesses, social media, etc.

I didn't really know much about any of that. I knew I had seen a few guys in the golf space on YouTube posting videos, but I wasn't really watching YouTube or using social media much at this time.

But from watching them talk so passionately about these topics, I was sold that this was the direction things were moving.

So after watching a bunch of their videos, I decided I wanted to try YouTube. Maybe this was something I could do. I went out and spent a few hundred dollars on what I thought was a "fancy" camera at the time. I got the camera a few weeks later and was all excited to start. Here we go, I thought—let's make some videos.

Well, I didn't know the first thing about cameras or making videos. I knew so little, in fact, that that first day with the camera, I couldn't even figure out how to get it to record. Eight years of YouTube videos later and I still laugh at that— I couldn't even get the camera to work.

The day I decided I wanted to try YouTube and got the camera to start filming was on a TUESDAY. I remember that day because just TWO DAYS LATER, on Thursday of that same week, one of my coaching clients—Mary— happened to come in for her weekly golf lesson.

The timing of her regular lesson just so happened to be right at the end of those group practices I mentioned earlier. This particular group lesson was one I did with my junior and competitive golfers.

We would have 10 to 20 kids from middle school to college age, all practicing together, music playing, competitions going on, jokes left and right. It was a FUN environment to see.

Well, Mary happened to see it, and before the end of our lesson that day, she made an offhand comment that "we should make a show out of this."

I almost couldn't believe the timing.

"That's funny," I said. "I don't know about a show, but I have been thinking of trying out this YouTube thing and making videos."

One thing led to the next, and I now had my first business partner!

Mary and I have gone on to produce more than 2,000 golf videos together since that day.

All three of those elements just happened to be at the right time and combined to lead us to start our online business:

1. I was burnt out.

2. I got exposed to those personal development guys talking about building online brands.

3. I met my partner who was willing to build it with us.

CHAPTER 6

The Early Years Online

Now we didn't go from 0 to 2,000 videos overnight, and it wasn't all roses along the way.

I didn't hear this quote at the time, but it's one I love now from John Maxwell that perfectly explains the process of building anything.

He holds his arm at an angle to show an uphill slope and he says, "Everything worthwhile is uphill."

I love this.

It's true.

Everything along our process has been uphill, but I'll tell ya what—it's been worth it. It's all been worth it. I would do it all over again, and it DOES get easier over time as YOU GET BETTER.

OUR FIRST YEAR

Our first year online: after an entire year of work, we made a grand total of $235.79.

(INSERT YOUTUBE SCREENSHOT)

We learned as we went.

Mary got the equipment and figured out how to use it all. Mary had a background in PR, so she knew media but didn't have any experience filming or editing.

So, we were both learning as we went.

We weren't exactly sure at that time what we were doing nor what it would lead to, but we both thought there was something there.

I knew moving things online was the way to go and it would only be shifting more and more in that direction, and we should get in there (semi) early. And she had enough faith in me and her abilities that together we could build this thing.

In the beginning, when we started this, I was still coaching full-time. I didn't have any extra time to devote to filming (so I thought), so the only thing we could figure out was to actually film me doing my lessons.

This would serve as our first type of content; it solved the time issue and gave out "real" coaching content, which I was dead set on as the best way to go.

We started filming and posting about once per week to start (you can still see our first video on Jan 1, 2017). We filmed, edited, posted…and no one watched.

Now, I didn't know at this time that this was normal—that when just about everyone starts, no one watches. So, it was tough in those early days. Knowing what I know now, I would have felt much better knowing it takes time and you build up momentum and views over time.

In fact, I tell people now that you need to look at your first 100 posts as just practice. You gotta just get through your first 100.

If you are posting once per week, that means two years of posting until I would really judge myself too much or start expecting any results.

But I/we didn't know that.

So those early months, I was discouraged often.

This is where having a partner, to me, was so important and the best thing I could have ever done.

I think there's a very real chance I would have quit in those early days if it was not for Mary.

I had a decent coaching business going; sure, I was feeling burnt out, but I could always just fall back on my lessons.

Mary was all in on us doing this and just wouldn't let us quit; thank God.

Now, I was all hell-bent on using real lessons as the videos in the beginning because I thought it was the best content.

I didn't know anything at this point about the importance of titles, thumbnails, hooks, b-roll, keeping the audience engaged, etc. (more on that later).

All I was focused on was giving great lessons, and I thought that was enough.

Well, it wasn't getting us results.

Those first sets of videos would get 5, 10, 20, 30 views per video, and only because I was sharing them with my Facebook audience.

Slowly we went from 20-30 views to about 100, then 200-300. So we were getting some traction on there beyond just our friends, family, and peers.

That was better; it was something, but it still wasn't enough.

Now, during these first months, Mary said to me several times that we should try "tip" style videos, like "how to":

How to drive the ball longer

How to fix your slice, etc.

I was dead against that.

I thought that was "clickbait" type stuff and wouldn't actually work. I thought the golfers needed to see real coaching; frankly, I thought it was stupid and that I was above it.

Well, after another few months of not a lot of results and no money, I had had enough.

That's it, I thought!

I've had enough of doing these videos and no one watching.

So one weekend, I decided I was going to go online and see what the people in the golf space that were actually getting views were doing.

It was clear very quickly that Mary was right.

They were doing tip style videos.

And not only were they doing tip style videos, but they were also using much different titles and thumbnails.

Much more clickbait style — much sexier.

Ours were very literal.

Here's an example:

They would use something like, "How To Gain 30 Yards Instantly With This One Driver Trick."

We would use something like, "Helping Nick Hit His Driver."

Their thumbnail would have some eye-catching images and text to go along with the sexy title, while ours were just a random image of me and the student during the lesson.

It was clear we needed to make some changes.

So, our very next shoot happened to be in the early spring of year two, right when the golf season was starting.

After a full year of the lesson videos, we were more than ready to try a new format.

So that's what we did.

We filmed three new videos—all tip style videos, all with more enticing titles and thumbnails—and BOOM! That was it.

We started to grow immediately, from those 100-300 view videos to 1,000-5,000 views on these.

I remember that right after that, we quickly hit our first 10,000 view video (this was early 2018), and still to this day, that was one of the most exciting things we have ever had happen.

10,000 people, I thought. WOW! That's when I knew we were really on to something and this was going to work.

We continued this strategy throughout the summer and fall and started to get much more traction.

Year 1 YouTube Results

768 Subscribers Gained

$235.79 Revenue

119,000 Views

Year 2 YouTube Results

32,800 Subscribers Gained

$17,965.62 Revenue

4,800,000 Views

You can see we started to gain a lot of momentum in the spring and rode that throughout the entire year.

Then something really important happened during the middle of that second year....

CHAPTER 7

Discovering The Dream Life Vision

I kept watching those Jim Rohn personal development videos and came across one of his "goal setting" workshops.

Now, up until this point in my life, I never really set any goals. I didn't really know about goal setting. I had some general ideas of what I wanted to do and what direction I wanted to move, but I never really took the time to focus on them, nor did I ever write them down.

Well, one day, as I was watching Jim's videos just like normal, I happened to see a video pop up of his that was titled "Jim Rohn Goal Setting Workshop."

It was about an hour-long, two-part video series.

I thought I may as well watch it and see what it was all about.

And this one was awesome, just like all the other of his other videos, but this was the first time I had actually seen him walk you through goal setting.

I had heard him mention goal setting in other videos but never how to do it.

It was a follow-along type of video where he would talk you through what to do step-by-step.

He called it your "Dream Life Vision"—what you would want your life to look like in 3, 5, 10, or 20 years from now if you could have whatever you want.

I had never done this before.

Admittedly, I watched the video once or twice before I actually pulled out a piece of paper, like Jim suggested, and actually wrote this stuff down.

He said to sit with a piece of paper and write down everything you could dream of: what do you want your life to look like in all areas.

Capture all the details.

Where do you live?

With whom?

How much money do you make?

Houses? Cars?

Etc.

It was really the first time I can remember where I allowed my mind to go to those places and think about what life could potentially look like.

Now, I made a critical error that first time around and did my list based on what I thought was realistic—what I could actually get based on my life at that time.

He mentioned again and again to do this exercise with no limits. Don't worry about what you think you can or cannot get or do. Think big—write it all down.

FinallyI did that. I let myself dream. What would my dream life look like?

I came up with some things at that time that seemed like they would be awesome to me:

- An awesome house in PA for the summers
- A beach house in Ocean City, Maryland
- A house in Florida near the beach for winters
- A Porsche 911
- A Range Rover
- A membership to an incredible country club

Things like this—just all material stuff first.

I wrote that list of about a page full of "stuff"—things I would want or how my life would be.

Then Jim said to write next to each one of those a 1, 3, 5, or 10.

That would indicate how long you thought it would take to get those.

So, I followed his lead and did that.

Then he said something that seemed small in the moment but proved to be huge and led to the big increases in my income in the coming years.

He said, "It should be everyone's goal to live their dream life with complete financial freedom."

He said "financial freedom" means you make enough money every month from your personally invested assets to pay for your dream lifestyle.

Woah!

This was a concept I had never heard or thought about before. So, you're telling me not only could I live my dream life, but there's always a way to do it where I could pay for all of that through my investments and not have to work?

Jim said the goal and the point of financial freedom is to get your expenses covered so you don't need to work to pay the bills. Your bills are already getting paid, so now you can work as you choose. When you want, how much you want, on what you want, with whom you want.

This lit a huge fire in me.

He said to go down your list of dream life things you wrote down and now next to them write what each of those would cost.

Now, keeping in mind this was 2018, before the pandemic and the big inflation that came in the following years, I looked up the houses, the cars, the country clubs, and everything on that list and calculated it would cost about $20,000 per month to pay for that lifestyle at the time.

On one hand, I was pleased with that; $20,000 per month didn't seem that bad—it wasn't a million per month. On the other hand, I was only making around $7,000 per month at the time and was already feeling maxed out and burnt out.

How the hell could I get to $20,000? That seemed like miles away.

As I did this exercise a few more times and got out of my head, I stopped trying to be realistic. I stopped thinking about how I would get these things and just let myself dream.

I thought, what the hell, let's see what this financial freedom would look like.

I knew I needed $20,000 per month to live this dream life.

That means I needed $240,000 in cash every year from my investments to cover that cost.

At this time, I had a grand total of $0 invested.

So, I needed to do some math to see how much money I would need invested to earn me $240,000 per year.

Again, keep in mind that at this time, I was making $80,000 per year (before expenses and taxes). So the idea of making $240,000 per year after taxes from just investments that didn't require me to actually go to work seemed like a pipe dream.

But I did the math anyway.

I searched around a bit, and while I saw varying figures, it seemed like a 6% return was a conservative amount to use based on my research.

So, $240,000 divided by a 6% return gave me $4,000,000.

I needed to get $4,000,000 invested to return me $240,000 per year, or $20,000 per month, for me to be able to live that dream lifestyle with complete financial freedom.

I'll never forget the feeling I got when I first wrote that number down.

On one hand, that $4,000,000 might as well have been $100 billion—it felt so far away. But on the other hand, it was the first time that it actually felt real.

My dream and thoughts that felt so crazy were now just a number on a piece of paper.

I was motivated!

Immediately after that, I remembered how Jim would always say a goal isn't a goal without a timeline. You need to put a timeframe and deadline on the goal.

Okay, I thought. I've got zero; I need to get to $4,000,000. How long do I want to give myself?

Around this time, I was about to turn 30 years old. So I thought, how about if we use a nice round number and try to accomplish it by 40?

That gives me 10 years.

Wouldn't it be cool to be 40 and living my dream life with complete financial freedom?

Hell yeah, I thought. I remembered Jim and others say several times that we often overestimate what we think we can do in one year, but we underestimate what we can accomplish in three years.

If that was true, then maybe I could do this in 10!

So I needed to do some more math.

I've got zero, and I need $4,000,000. Now I know I have 10 years to do it.

Since we were just starting to make a little bit of money online, I didn't think it would be fair to just divide it by 10 years.

$4,000,000 divided by 10 years means I needed to save $400,000 per year starting that year. I was only making $80,000; how the hell could I save $400,000?

I went back to that Jim Rohn quote, "we overestimate what we can do in one year, but we underestimate what we could do in three years."

So, I gave myself the first three years to build my income and business up—this year and the next two.

I now needed $4,000,000 and only seven years to save it. This meant I would need to save about $560,000 per year from the time I did the math until my 40th birthday.

I figured I might as well factor in living my dream life the whole time along the way and paying $240,000 for that. You add those together: ($560,000 savings) + ($240,000 living) and you get $800,000. Now you add taxes to that (I factored in a 33% tax rate), and that gives you $1,200,000. I needed to make $1,200,000 per year every year for the next ten years to get my $4,000,000.

I had the same exact feelings as when I first saw the $4,000,000 number.

On one hand, I thought that number again might as well have been a billion dollars. I was making $80,000; how the hell would I get to $1,200,000?

On the other hand, it got me excited. Again, it made it real for me. I had a number, I had a target, I had a goal, and I had a clear vision.

Now that I had my clear vision and was excited to get going, I had to figure out how I would actually do this.

After I got over my shock and awe of the number and how far away I was, I remembered hearing a couple of Tony Robbins videos I had watched where he talked about modeling success. Once I discovered Jim Rohn was Tony Robbins' mentor, I went back to that very first video my friend sent me and started watching all of his content.

He said one of the best ways to figure out what to do or how to start is to model success.

Okay, I thought; that makes sense. Without knowing it, ironically, it turns out that's exactly what we did with our YouTube videos to start getting some traction.

We weren't getting results with our lesson-style videos, so we went and looked at what the successful people in our space were doing, and we modeled them. Not copied, but modeled success. We modeled their video styles, their topics, their titles, and their thumbnails.

So now, as I was trying to figure out how to build a business that makes me $1,200,000 per year, I wanted to use the same strategy and find people I could model for this as well.

So first, I thought, is there anyone in my golf space who makes $1,200,000 per year?

I wasn't sure, but I knew of some coaches who I thought were definitely successful and seemed to be earning much more money than me.

I looked at their coaching models and what they were doing and saw there were only two main things they did to create much more revenue:

1. In-person golf schools

2. Online membership sites

Okay, so it was possible.

Then I thought, outside of golf, is there anyone else who makes $1,200,000?

This I was more certain of—definitely yes.

How about people outside of my space but who do coaching or online businesses like I could?

Again, a definite yes. As I had been watching Gary Vaynerchuck and Grant Cardone, I had been exposed to a bunch of people they would talk about and showcase who were also crushing it online and making millions of dollars per year in that space.

Okay, I thought, if someone else could do it, so could we.

We had a clear vision, and now we could model success.

At this very time, again seemingly with amazing timing, once I went through those exercises:

- Came up with my dream life vision
- Did the math
- Came up with the $4M and $1.2M targets
- Figured out how we could model success
- Saw that the two main options were golf schools or membership sites

I was just getting done with all of this, I happened to get an email from two guys saying they were big fans of me and my golf content and were reaching out because they were interested in building a membership site with a golf pro and thought we would be a perfect fit.

Are you kidding me?

Now, does it make sense that they would reach out around this time AFTER we had just stated to get some videos to gain traction and started to gain an audience? Of course.

They wouldn't have reached out in year one when no one was watching.

So the timing of them reaching out outside of the timing relative to us coming up with the dream life vision still would make sense.

And I could buy that—but I've had similar situations happen too often for me to think that timing was just by accident.

So we talked back and forth for a while and decided we would build our membership site, and www.cogornogolf.com was launched in October 2018, toward the end of that second year when we were gaining some traction.

During that first year online, when we didn't make any money, I had some serious doubts. But now, by the end of the second year, we were gaining some momentum and seeing results.

While my income stayed at the same $80,000 mark during my last year of in-person coaching and our first year online, during year two online, I saw a nice jump from roughly $80,000 to roughly $150,000.

Some of this came from that $17,965 YouTube AdSense revenue; some came from our membership site launch, and some came from my prices going up again.

In year one on YouTube, not only did we not make any money, but I didn't get a single person coming to get a lesson from the videos.

But in year two, that all changed.

I started to get people coming in right away in the spring when those videos started to pop off.

I noticed people first coming from my local area, within about an hour or so away—and at that time, that was a big deal.

I had only given lessons to people in my local area (say within 20 minutes or so), so when people started to come up from the Philadelphia area, about an hour and 30 minutes away, I was blown away.

Then some people started driving from 3–4 hours away. I was shocked.

Then my first clients flew in from across the country. I couldn't believe it.

Then, by the end of the year, I had people fly in from all over the world (Australia, Germany, and Japan even) to little old

Bethlehem, Pennsylvania, just to see me for some golf lessons?

Wow! We were really on to something. Not only were the videos getting some traction now, but people started coming in from all over the world to get coaching from me.

There was more to this online YouTube and social media stuff than I realized.

Maybe—just maybe—we could actually pull off this dream life thing.

Fast forward five years, and we have been able, at the time of this writing, to grow our coaching revenues to over $1,500,000 in revenue, with over $1,000,000 in profit.

I learned a lot about growing our social media, building our audience, monetizing that audience, and scaling it that I want to share with you next.

CHAPTER 8

Building Your Audience Online (Why It Matters)

From a business perspective, building our AUDIENCE is one of the KEY fundamental requirements for us to make more money.

To increase our revenues, we either need to sell MORE to the same amount of people we already have, or sell our stuff to MORE people.

That's really it in terms of how we make more money.

We make more money PER CURRENT CUSTOMER, or we get MORE/NEW CUSTOMERS.

How do we get more/new customers?

We need to increase our audience—increase the number of people who KNOW US that we can get our offer in front of.

Now, the whole idea in terms of increasing our audience is to GO WHERE THE PEOPLE ARE.

In today's age, that's social media.

Back in the day, that was once radio, TV, newspapers, and commercials; all of those still CAN work, but every day that passes means more and more of our audience is on social media.

We want to meet them where they are, and so that's where we decided to focus and where we are going to focus on moving forward.

I remember Grant Cardone saying over and over again in those personal development videos that I was watching that we needed to GET ATTENTION—that money only FLOWS to you when people KNOW YOU.

How is someone supposed to give you money if they don't even know you exist, he used to say.

That made sense to me.

Now, when you are looking to grow your audience online, there are TWO main strategies you can start with:

1. ORGANIC

2. PAID

You can either use ORGANIC (non-paid, no ads) to grow your audience.

This would be posting on your social media accounts and growing your audience organically.

Paid would mean using ads or buying email lists or things like that.

Neither is RIGHT or WRONG.

Organic is easier to do in the sense that there are no barriers to entry.

You don't need money to use for the ads or have to know how to run paid ads or anything like that.

Organic is the strategy we decided to use to grow our socials, so that's what we are going to focus on here.

Having a bigger audience has a few big benefits:

1. It enables you to use the supply and demand curve in your favor to charge higher prices for your existing coaching (I'll show you how I did that next).

2. It builds you a list of potential customers for your new ONLINE offers.

3. Down the road, it enables you to create other "passive" revenue sources like YouTube AdSense, affiliates, sponsorships, etc.

Here's a quick example of how the math could work to show you how much more money you can make from an increased audience alone, BEFORE actually making any money online.

Let's use my early years in Bethlehem as an example.

Let's say about 500 people knew who I was in my area—they knew me, who I was, and that I taught golf.

Let's say I started at $30/hr coaching, which I did, and let's say I was able to fill 20 hours per week coaching.

$30/hour X 20 hours = $600 per week.

$600 per week X 4 weeks = $2,400 per month revenue (small audience revenue).

Now fast forward to today, where millions of people per MONTH watch our videos.

So, 500 people who knew me when I started led to $2,400 per month revenue.

Now, by just changing ONE thing (a bigger audience), let's see what the math looks like when millions of people now know me.

I went from a $30/hour lesson rate to $350/hour (from that audience growth).

Let's use the same example of 20 hours per week and say we kept our coaching amounts (supply) the same.

$350/hour X 20 hours = $7,000 per week.

$7,000 per week X 4 weeks = $28,000 per month revenue (big audience revenue).

Think about that.

From $2,400 per month to $28,000 per month.

Same guy.

Same job.

Almost a 12X increase in my rates, all from ONE thing: a bigger audience—more people knowing who I am.

Now, I think that's SO POWERFUL to see. Of course, we are going to talk about the different ways we (and you can) monetize that audience to create additional revenue sources.

But even if that NEVER happened, is it WORTH the energy to create the content and build the audience?

Hell yes.

I'd much rather have $28,000 per month than $2,400, and I'm sure you would too.

So let's talk next about HOW to actually build your audience, and then we'll go over how to monetize that audience online as well after that.

Because not only did we go from $2,400/month to $28,000/month just from raising our in-person rates due to this increase in audience, we also went from $80,000 per year to $1,500,000 per year once we learned how to make money online ON TOP OF that in-person coaching!

CHAPTER 9

Build Your Audience Online (How To Actually Do It)

1. Go where they are and pick the top 1-2 platforms

This is one I mentioned already, but it's important enough to mention again.

I learned a lot on this topic from Gary Vaynerchuk about going where people are putting their attention.

There's nothing special about social media compared to other media sources; it's simply WHERE people are currently spending their time and energy, so we want to make sure we are visible there.

Now, there are A LOT of different types of social media to pick from:

- YouTube
- Instagram
- Facebook
- LinkedIn
- TikTok

Just to name a few.

For some of the bigger guys who have TEAMS of people creating and posting content, it's more realistic to be on all platforms and in all places at once—posting multiple times per day on all of those platforms.

For us, when most of us are by ourselves or maybe have one other person helping us, it's simply not realistic to be on all platforms all at once and do it well.

Today, I have a team of about 10 people with 4 full-time people, so we are able to spread ourselves out across a bunch of platforms, but in those early years, there were just two of us.

Mary and I.

We decided to focus all of our energy on YouTube.

I had a small Instagram going, but it wasn't something we focused on more until later.

YouTube made sense; it's where a lot of our audience was.

Our target customer who takes golf lessons is generally males from 35 to 75 years old who have discretionary income.

Now, at this time, I was already coaching full time while filming our videos, and Mary had to do all of the filming, editing, thumbnails, posting, etc., for all the videos.

So, YouTube was enough.

I would pick ONE — maybe TWO — platforms to focus on to start.

Depending on your industry and where your potential customers spend time, I would prioritize that.

Maybe that's YouTube like us, maybe it's Instagram, or maybe LinkedIn.

We have had so much success going all in on YouTube that if I had to pick, I would live there. It takes more work, but the monetization opportunities are the best.

2. Long Term Mindset

When building your audience, you want to have a LONG-term perspective. Those examples I gave of $30 to $350 per hour took me 7 years to accomplish.

You could see from the revenue examples above that we posted for a full year without making any money.

It wasn't until year 2 and year 3 that we started to get more traction.

3. Consistent Posting

Not only do we want to have a long-term mindset, but we want to go in with a mindset that we are going to be EXTREMELY consistent with our posting.

The mantra that worked for us was "post 3 times per week, no matter what." No matter what.

We posted every Tuesday, Thursday, and Sunday at 10 AM EST for 6 years.

3 times per week. Same days. Same times; never missing a single post.

Now this doesn't GUARANTEE anything, but it sure does increase the odds of success, don't you think?

3 times per week... every week... for 6 years.

Part of the benefit at the time and as you're building your audience is that THEY (the audience) KNOW when you're going to post and are prepared for it. But honestly, it's more for the muscle, for the habit and discipline you build.

You can't just film and post WHEN YOU FEEL LIKE IT.

That isn't going to work.

I didn't feel like it A LOT of times.

You want to make an agreement with yourself for how often you can post, and again, think LONG TERM. Pick an amount and schedule that you can keep doing for a long time—think 3, 5, 10, 20 years.

Social media and building an online business is much more like running a marathon, not a sprint. It's not about how many you can post in your first week; it's how many weeks you can post for—week after week, month after month, year after year.

4. Make Each Set Better Than the Last

Now, posting on the right platforms with a long-term mindset and doing it consistently doesn't mean you're automatically going to be successful, but it's a hell of a start.

I think what does make your odds of success as close to 100% as possible is when you stack on this one on top of the first 3:

MAKE EACH SET OF VIDEOS BETTER THAN THE LAST

We started posting once per week for the first year. Then we increased to twice per week. Then 3 times per week.

Throughout that process, we would look at each set of videos and just try to make ONE thing better for the next set.

The compound effect of this over the course of a year (or years) is almost unbelievable.

This can be the smallest of things to improve, but something—things like:

- Better lighting
- Better delivery in the video
- Better b-roll
- Better titles
- Better thumbnails
- Better hook to start the video
- Better close to end the video

- Speak clearer in video
- Better topic
- Better energy in the video
- Better audio

Whatever it is; something little.

So, let's say for the first year you post once per week. That means each month you have 4 videos posted. Let's say you film all 4 of these at once.

You don't need to be in a huge rush here; remember it's a marathon.

So, say you post those 4 in the first month. Watch all of them and pick 1-2 things you can do better for the next round.

Maybe you improve the lighting and the audio.

Then you do another set next month with better audio and lighting. Then you watch the new set and see you can improve your hook at the start of the video and add better b-roll throughout.

Now you improve that the next month for the next set.

Then you see those 4 and realize you can improve the titles and thumbnails.

You see how this starts to add up?

You're only 3 months in, and already you have improved your lighting, audio, hooks, b-roll, titles, and thumbnails.

And for each of these, you may need to do a little research and work to figure out how to improve them. That's normal—that's why only 1-2 things per set, and only doing it weekly/monthly.

Before you know it, you're a professional content creator!

If you want to see our evolution with this and our SLOW but SURE progress, check out the videos on YouTube, "Eric Cogorno Golf," and start from oldest to newest.

5. Prioritize It In Your Schedule

I think in all areas of life this is true, and it certainly is in content creation.

If it's important to you, you need to prioritize it in your schedule.

Once we got past that first year or so of filming and posting my actual lessons, we started to actually DEVOTE SPECIFIC time to create the videos.

Once we changed to the "tip" style and I started seeing traction from it, I was more willing to block off some time where I wouldn't teach so that we had time to CREATE the content.

Now, we got away with it, but looking back now, that was a mistake—and I would do it differently if I had to go back and do it all over again.

I would block out time specifically to create content for social media right from the start.

Once we blocked out time, we decided to film on Mondays—the first day of the week; the first thing we did that week because it was the MOST IMPORTANT thing to our long-term growth of our business.

We have since filmed every Monday at 12 PM EST for the past 8 years, minus a few holidays.

During the period when we first went from 2-3 videos per week, we also added a Friday film day, but our main thing is every Monday.

We would film our 2-3 videos, meet, and discuss anything we needed to move the business forward. First thing of the week—every week.

So, I would look at your schedule and see where you may be able to fit this in.

Remember, if it's important to you, it shouldn't be squeezed in last minute; it certainly shouldn't be off the schedule where you only do it when you can.

Put it in.

My Mondays have been and will continue to be permanently blocked off for filming, no matter what.

6. Make Content That The AUDIENCE Wants, Not What You Want

This is one that took me a while to learn. Remember back during that first year when we were posting those lesson videos?

We did that because that's what I wanted to do.

I learned very quickly by the lack of response that that was not what the audience wanted.

The audience wanted the tip-style videos.

That was evidenced by the views on the videos going up and also from seeing what other successful people in the space were doing.

If you aren't sure WHAT they want, I would look at what other people in the space are doing that is working. What sort of content are they producing that is working well?

Watch all of their videos, but also READ THE COMMENTS.

There is so much gold in the comments of the videos from those other people in your space.

The audience will share what they like, questions they have, and videos they want to see, etc. Corporations pay A LOT of money to figure out what their audiences want via surveys and focus groups. We can get that all for FREE by reading the comments of the videos of successful people in our space.

7. Model Success

Not only should we model success when it comes to figuring out WHAT sort of content to make, but we should model success in all kinds of categories.

MODEL, not copy.

Back to that Tony Robbins quote from earlier that really stuck with me: model the success of others to figure out your PATH—how to start, what to do.

Obviously, we can model TOPICS and WHAT content we are doing, as mentioned above, but we can also model:

- Titles
- Thumbnails
- Video length
- How they intro the video
- How they deliver the main message
- How they close the video
- The style of the video
- Etc.

When it comes to modeling, you want to figure out what they are doing that's WORKING and do your own version of it.

So you can do a SIMILAR style video with a similar topic, but in your way—from your perspective, with your stories, etc.

We don't need to reinvent the wheel to make good content and build an audience; we just need to find a wheel that's rolling and roll along with it.

8. The First 100 Are Just Practice

This is a mindset that has REALLY helped me as time has gone on, and I think it's very useful when it comes to creating organic content on social media.

Especially if you are in the early phase of posting videos/content, think about your first 100 videos as purely practice.

I adopted this mindset for our new Personal Development channel, and it's super useful to keep things in perspective.

The first 100 are just practice.

Don't expect anyone to watch.

Don't expect any results.

Just show up. Build the habit of creating and posting the content.

Get through your first 100, and then your expectations can change.

And remember, we aren't just doing the first 100 and blindly posting them all; we are going to look at each set of videos and try to improve 1-2 things from the last set.

So, if you do one per week, 100 videos will take 2 years.

Every month you improve 1-2 things.

That means by the end of 2 years you will have improved 24-48 things about your videos.

I'm willing to bet your content not only will be much better, but the results you're getting and traction will come along with it.

You will be BUILDING YOUR AUDIENCE!

CHAPTER 10

YouTube Specific Strategies

Here are some specific things I've learned over the past 8 years that have helped us grow our YouTube channel from zero to over 300,000 subscribers.

YouTube has served as the CORE of our online growth strategy, and it can be credited for much of our success.

Obviously, it serves as its own revenue generator, but beyond that, it has been the main source we have used to funnel golfers to our membership site and other paid services.

We have been able to grow and KEEP our audience much the same as I built my in-person business—taking great care of them, trying to provide excellent service (content), having them tell their friends about us (word of mouth), asking them to subscribe and send to a friend (referrals), and keeping them engaged by focusing FIRST and FOREMOST on creating content that will HELP them get better at what they are there for.

These are some of the things that I've learned that helped us grow a lot from year 2-8:

1. Titles and Thumbnails Matter a Lot

In those early years, I put very little attention on the title and the thumbnail and ALL of my attention on the video itself.

Now, I had that half right; we DO need to put a lot of attention on making the video itself really good—the PRODUCT needs to be great. Just like with our coaching, the MOST important thing is that our COACHING is good; same with our videos—the most important thing is that our videos are GOOD. They need to provide a lot of value to the viewer and help them with what they are there for.

But I learned really quickly that you can have the best videos in the world and if no one watches them, then it doesn't matter—you didn't help anyone!

You ever heard the popular phrase from the old Field of Dreams movie: "If you build it, they will come"?

Yeah, that doesn't apply to social media.

We need to build it and figure out how the hell to get them there.

Now, with social media, how we get them there is by getting their attention.

How do we do that?

With great TITLES and THUMBNAILS to make them STOP and CLICK.

What titles and thumbnails should you be using?

Use the advice above and model success. See what the successful people in your space are doing that is working and model (don't copy) off of that!

A GREAT title and THUMBNAIL can 10-100x the views on the SAME video versus a worse title and thumbnail.

You'll get better at this as you go, but remember the goal here is to get ATTENTION—to grab someone's attention when they are scrolling that will make them click and watch.

It needs to be a topic they are interested in, of course (that's the TOPIC part you need to get good at), but the title and thumbnail should bring up INTRIGUE and CURIOSITY, creating a desire to click and find out more.

This is a never-ending game to improve and adapt over time, but you'll get better at this with practice.

2. My Sunday/Monday Prep and Film Process

What worked really well for us was making sure we prepped for the videos beforehand and had as much pre-production work done as possible.

That means we didn't just show up to film and say, "OK, what are we talking about today?"

Maybe some people can do that well, but for us, preparation helped a lot.

We already talked about the importance of making content creation a priority and putting it in your schedule, so we would film every Monday at 12 PM EST.

That meant every Sunday, the day before (on my one "off" day per week), I would prepare for the following day's filming.

I would spend 2-4 hours generally the day before doing this prep work.

Figuring out:

- What topic will we cover?
- What will be my main message points?
- What will be the title?
- What's the thumbnail?
- How will we intro/start the video?
- How will we close/call to action?

I would keep a running list of potential topics in the "notes" section of my phone, so anytime I thought of something that would be good for a video, I would put it in there, or if something happened during my lessons that I thought would make a good video, I'd put it in there.

So, I would reference that list.

In the beginning years, when you haven't done ANY videos before, you have a bunch of "evergreen" videos on topics you need to do for the first time. That part is pretty easy, but once you get through that list, you need to get a bit more creative.

Here again is where you can model success.

I would watch (and still do) what everyone else is posting that is having success in my space.

What are the topics? Titles, thumbnails, intros, main points in videos, creative points of views, and the audience's reaction in the comments?

This will always give you great info, ideas, and general directions you can move with your content.

So by the time we actually film the video, I've already got an outline for the topic, the title, the thumbnails, the intro, and the close.

I will have rehearsed the video 2-3 times in my head throughout the day, just to work out the details.

I never liked to script the videos word for word, but I also didn't like to wing it, so I would just have a very general outline I would write on a legal pad with the title, a few bullet points I wanted to mention, and any main points I wanted to make.

So there were lots of freedoms within the outline/video for me to riff, but still within the structure of the video.

No winging it.

Prep every Sunday.

Film every Monday.

Try and make each set of videos better than the last.

That was the main recipe from 0 to 300,000 on our journey.

3. Actual Meat/Content Outline

In terms of the actual content of the video, I have learned that usually LESS is more.

I want to have like ONE overarching message for the video.

As an example, we would do something like "HOW TO HIT YOUR DRIVER FARTHER," so there was ONE main thing/message: hitting your driver farther.

Then I would have 2-3 sub-concepts/strategies on how to accomplish the main thing.

So, as an example, maybe the video was "How to Hit Your Driver Farther," and the 3 main concepts to achieve that would be:

1. Have more tilt at setup
2. Turn more in the backswing
3. Hit more up on the ball

Something like that. I would explain the one main message and the 2-3 sub-concepts or strategies to get it.

That's the MEAT.

The general video structure will go like this:

A. There's an intro/hook (what they are going to learn and why it's going to help them)

B. The MEAT of the video (what you are teaching them)

C. A summary (what they learned and why it's important)

D. A close/call-to-action (CTA) Tell them what to do next—like watch the next video or go to your website to sign up for coaching

4. The HOOK/INTRO

This is the beginning part of the video. You've got their attention through your title and thumbnail enough to make them click.

Now you want to GRAB their attention AGAIN and KEEP their attention.

We want to confirm they are going to get what they clicked on the video for—what they are about to get and why it's so important for them to watch and how it's going to help them.

This could be in the 7-30-60 second range. The first 5, 10, or 30 seconds of the video are where A LOT of people who clicked will decide if they want to stay and keep watching or not.

So we want to make sure it looks good. We lead with excitement and passion for what we are going to talk about.

5. Choose Topics the Audience Wants

This was a lesson I learned the hard way during that first year and a half going from lesson clips to tip-style videos.

Just like any business, we have to give the customer what the customer wants — not what WE WANT.

To figure out what kind of product to sell, we would need to determine what kind of product the customer wants.

The same applies for videos; we are selling something, and that's our content.

Don't make the mistake I made creating videos that I WANTED; do the videos your AUDIENCE wants.

How do we figure out WHAT they want?

You guessed it…model success! What are the topics other successful people in your space are getting a lot of people to watch?

That's your answer.

6. The Close/Call To Action

We always want to lead our audience somewhere at the end of the video. What should they do next?

Do we want them to stay on YouTube and watch another video?

Or do we want them to go to your site and sign up for coaching?

I would always make sure I have a clear idea of what I want them to do after the video BEFORE we even create the video!

Then at the end, you tell them what to do.

If you want them to watch another video, know what that video is ahead of time and say something like, "OK, if you liked this video, you're going to LOVE this one where I talk about _____. We'll put that on the screen. Go ahead and click that and watch that now!"

Or if you want them to go to your site, you can say something like, "OK, if this video helped you and you want to improve EVEN MORE, go to _____ (your site) now and get your free 14-day trial to my _____ program before it closes on _____ date!"

7. The 80/20 Rule

Once you start to get some videos under your belt, especially once you get past that first 100, you'll start to find out what is working and what isn't.

Naturally, you can adapt and lean more into what is working and stop doing what isn't working.

I've found a pretty good rule of thumb for this that has worked for us: spend about 80% of the time continuing to do more of what is currently working and about 20% of the time testing/trying new stuff.

The 20% new could be something VERY small like a title, thumbnail, intro, etc., or it could be something bigger like a totally different format.

So, if you do 5 videos in a month, 4 of them can be doubling down on what has been working and 1 would be testing/trying something new; again, this applies to one little micro thing in your video or the video as a whole.

8. Content Types

I mentioned this before, but I would consider which of the 3 main content type buckets you want to live in:

A. HOW TO talking head style—You talking about a topic, explaining and demonstrating.

B. Document—Recording you actually doing the thing.

C. Story tell—Talking about what you did.

See what you like best, what you are the best at, but ultimately which style your audience wants the most and lean into that. You'll figure this out with a little bit of trial and error pretty quickly.

9. Posting Frequency

More isn't necessarily better here, but not enough isn't good either.

We built our channel by posting progressively more and then finding a middle ground:

- Year 1: we posted once per week.

- Year 2: we posted twice per week.

- Year 3: we posted three times per week plus went live every Monday night.

- Year 4: same as Year 3.

- Year 5: we posted three times per week but stopped the live.

- Year 6: same as Year 5.

- Year 7: we tested posting 1-2 times per week and saw better results.

- Year 8: we continued with 1-2 times per week.

See what works best for you and produces the best results, but with YouTube in particular, I would think no less than once per week.

A lot of people in the coaching/services space have built great channels and businesses on one video per week.

Start with that: pick a day and time and stick with that weekly posting time no matter what.

You can test more frequent posting over time as you build some momentum, make your videos better, learn what works, and potentially get a bigger team to help produce.

10. Additional Revenue Sources (AdSense, Affiliates, Sponsors)

What's really great about YouTube compared to the other platforms is how you can monetize on the platform.

While there is a longer list of ways you could do this, these would be the big three I would look at:

AdSense

Not only can you build your audience FOR FREE (we don't have to pay to use YouTube), but YouTube will pay you AdSense, which is a percentage of the money advertisers pay them to run ads on your videos (I believe it's a 55/45% split).

We have built that AdSense from zero to around $150,000/year profit.

Affiliates

Another awesome way you can monetize your audience is through affiliate marketing relationships. Now, you can do this on other platforms as well, but we did this mainly on YouTube.

This is where you find a product or service in your space that your audience wants that you can PROMOTE and SELL to them and get a percentage of the sales.

An example for us would be a golf training aid (something they can use to help fix their swing).

Another company makes the product, so we don't own it, but we make an agreement with that company so that we can promote it and sell it to our audience.

Let's say it costs $100 for the product, and we get a 30% commission. So, for every unit someone from our audience buys using the link we give them, we make $30.

If you can find the RIGHT affiliates with the right product/offer that your audience loves, you can do a lot here.

We have built our affiliates from zero to over $100,000/year profit.

Sponsors

Once you have built a large enough audience and gained more traction and views, you can start securing sponsorships.

This would be other companies paying you to USE their product in your videos, or promote their products in your videos, or a combination of both.

In the golf space, we have had sponsors from clothing, hats, shoes, golf clubs, hydration products, etc., that would pay us to wear, use, or feature their products in our videos.

We have built our sponsorships from zero to over $100,000/year profit.

CHAPTER 11

Bridging The Gap Between Building Our Audience And Monetizing the Audience

The GAP we need to bridge once we are consistently creating content, getting past our first 100 posts, and making minor improvements on each set is to make sure we achieve something called "PERCEIVED EXPERTISE."

The people watching our videos need to PERCEIVE US as experts in our space.

You may have heard before that people buy from people they "know, like, and trust."

The KNOWING part we already talked about. Remember the Grant Cardone quote? Money only flows to you if someone knows you.

We get people to KNOW us through building our audience—through either posting organically or paid marketing.

Once they KNOW us, how do we get them to LIKE and TRUST us?

There are several variables involved in the LIKE part, but a lot of this we can gain from showing our PERSONALITY and PASSION.

People like people they can relate to—people whose personality they like, people with good vibes, people who are honest, people who are vulnerable, and people who bring energy and passion to the topic.

Think to yourself when you see content from someone or meet someone in person, and you think to yourself, "I like that guy."

What is it about that guy that you like?

We want to show that off in our content in our own unique ways—not faking it, but being authentically ourselves.

OKAY, so they get to KNOW us from our content, and they get to LIKE us from HOW we are in our content, but how do they TRUST us?

This is where PERCEIVED EXPERTISE comes in.

It's easier to build TRUST with someone in person, but when we are talking ONLINE through video or text, it's a bit different.

We trust other people online that we have never met when we PERCEIVE them to be experts in their space. That they know what they are talking about and can PROVE IT. So, that's what we need to do—know what we are actually talking about and be able to prove it.

How do we do this?

1. Actually be great at coaching or the thing you do (remember that from before). We can't fake this; you need to actually be good.

2. Demonstrate that we truly know what we are talking about with our content style by explaining topics, showing us doing the thing, or showing us working/having worked with someone else who did the thing.

There are THREE main content styles that I like to use for this:

1. "HOW TO" talking head

- This is where it's YOU in the video explaining something—explaining a topic.

2. Documenting

- This is where YOU record YOU doing the thing—yourself or with a client.

3. Storytelling

- This is where you tell a story about you doing the thing or doing it with a client.

Here's an example of how I would use each of these: let's say with the topic of how to hit the golf ball farther.

1. HOW TO" Talking Head

- I would create a video explaining how to hit the ball farther—I would talk to the camera and demonstrate what I'm talking about. I would have 1-3 main bullet points as to HOW to hit the ball farther that I would explain and demonstrate.

2. Documenting

- I would record a lesson of me teaching one of my students how to hit it farther by doing those same 1-3 main bullet points. I would document what I was actually doing.

3. Storytelling

- I would tell a story of how I was able to gain distance myself or how I got a student to gain distance using those 1-3 main bullet points.

Since we aren't able to meet these people in person and the only context they see us through is our content, we can DISPLAY our EXPERTISE—our knowledge and our abilities—through these content types.

Then they will have found us, liked us for who we are, and trusted us for what we know and demonstrate.

NOW, we are ready to make them an offer and monetize.

CHAPTER 12

How To Monetize Your Online Audience

1. Figure out What You Want to Offer

What is the thing that you want to offer to or sell to your audience?

Assuming we are in the coaching or service-based industries, we will likely sell our coaching or services.

We started by selling my coaching in those early days—first on Instagram selling "online lessons" and then on YouTube.

I had learned enough through my in-person coaching to know to offer "packages" versus one-off lessons.

So, I started with packages of online coaching—monthly prices for a certain amount of lessons per month, plus feedback in between the sessions.

I thought to myself, "How can I make my first $1,000 online?"…

2. Start with a Plan to Make Your First $1,000 Per Month and Build From There

I really like this as a starting point.

Something small and achievable that we can ALL do—get some momentum, make some sales, figure out the details of your offer, practice online coaching, get some customer success, and build some income along the way.

So, whatever you're selling (let's say your coaching), how could you make your first $1,000 per month?

For me, starting on Instagram and some YouTube, I began by offering a $100/month plan where they got 2 online lessons per month.

I thought, "OK, let's see if I can sell 10 people into a $100/month plan, which would get me to $1,000."

Now, there are hundreds of golf coaches selling lessons online, so there is much more to model now. But at the time, there weren't that many, so I wasn't sure what the market would be for these.

I was charging around $100/hour for my in-person lessons at that time, so I thought, "OK, I know people are willing to exchange that amount for in-person—let's try half of that for online": $100/month for 2 lessons and feedback in between.

I started to pitch this in my videos and SLOWLY but surely got some sales.

Two people signed up within the first week, so I had $200/month of new revenue.

Then 4-5 people came in, then 7-8, and finally, within 3 months, I got my first 10.

I had created my first $1,000/month in online sales.

I was pumped! It was the first time I was making money from coaching outside of my in-person lessons.

Now, it's important to note that I didn't just create this coaching offer and leave a link for them to sign up. I needed to go out and TALK ABOUT my offer—A LOT—just to get those first ten, which leads me to...

3. Put a CALL TO ACTION in All of Your Content

If you've been paying attention, you'll notice we have a theme going on here with the "everything doesn't just take care of itself" lesson that I learned.

Well, that was no different when I first launched my online coaching. Unless you're a unicorn, it will be the same for you.

This is true no matter what, but especially the earlier you are in the process, the smaller the audience you have, or the less perceived expertise you have.

Your offer (your coaching) IS NOT GOING TO SELL ITSELF.

YOU need to sell it—actively. Just like I did.

What that means is you need to talk about it. A lot.

You need to make your audience aware of your offer first things first. Remember, if they don't know you, they can't flow money to you. The same applies for your offer. If they don't know about your coaching offer, how are they supposed to sign up and pay you?

So, we need to make them aware of it—often.

We all see SO MUCH on social media nowadays and throughout our lives that we forget things. We need to CONSTANTLY remind them that we are here, we are great at our coaching, and we have a way to help them achieve their goals.

Let them know about the offer and what their lives will look like after they make those transformations with you and your coaching (why they NEED to get it).

During the early days of Instagram, I would mention this in the text description of EVERY post I was doing about 3 times per week.

Later on YouTube, when we started our membership site, we could mention it in EVERY VIDEO—3 times per week.

So, 6 times per week, we were mentioning our coaching offer to the audience.

4. Learn the Give/Ask Ratio

Gary Vaynerchuk really popularized this and made me aware of it with his "Jab, Jab, Jab, Right Hook" mantra and book.

Give, Give, Give, Ask.

In his book, he said it should really be Jab, Jab, Jab, Jab, Jab, Jab, Jab…Right Hook.

This means give, give, give, ask.

The jabs are the GIVE.

The right hook is the offer (asking for the sale).

We want to be GIVING our audience FREE, HELPFUL content to help them ALL THE TIME—content that is genuinely made to HELP THEM with whatever we are coaching.

But of course, we have a business to run and an offer to make in order to get people to sign up and buy our stuff.

So, what's the right ratio?

While I think FREQUENCY is key, we also want to keep things generally short and sweet.

For years on YouTube, we would make three 10-15 minute "how to" videos where I would be teaching people how to golf better.

So, with YouTube alone, that was 30-45 minutes of FREE, HELPFUL content each week.

I figured if we spent 30-60 seconds in each video pitching the site and explaining how it was going to really help them, that was an acceptable ratio.

30-45 minutes of content

1.5-3 minutes of promoting

Let's just use the high end to make the numbers simple.

45 minutes of free helpful content each week.

42 of those minutes were content.

3 minutes were promotion.

That's over 93% of the time we provided free helpful content, and just under 3% was dedicated to promotion.

I like that sort of ratio.

Of course, yours doesn't need to be the same, but I would aim for those sorts of zones for your content.

See what your total amount of weekly content is and then find out what about 3-5% of that time is and allocate that for promotion.

If it's LESS than that, you likely are not promoting your offer enough.

If you are MORE than that, you may be overdoing it.

With that ratio, we tried all sorts of timing for the promotion—the beginning, after 30 seconds, after 60 seconds, 2 minutes in, middle of the video, end of the video, etc.

See what works best for you. We've had varying amounts of success with each, but what we landed on 80% of the time was about 30-60 seconds in after the beginning.

So, we would either give them a hook (me talking about what the video was about and why it was important that they watch and how it was going to help them) for about 30-60 seconds.

Then it would go to a promo of the site for 30-60 seconds and then right into the content.

We would either do the hook or a preview of the best part of the video coming up to TEASE THEM.

While having the promo in the front part of the video CAN lose you viewers who will click off, it CAN also increase your sales amount. So that's something you need to play with, test, and find the right balance for you.

5. HOW TO GET PEOPLE IN TO START

Ultimately, we want to learn to craft an "irresistible offer," which we'll go over next, but I would fill your online offer really the same way I would fill your in-person offer.

The main strategy here is to offer something FREE for someone to try. Take away all of the risk for them.

Remember in the in-person coaching where I offered those "free lessons" on Saturdays, and then I would convert a percentage of those into paid coaching?

The same thing applies here.

One of the big reasons people DON'T buy (outside of those who just don't and will never want your services, coaching, or products) is that they aren't SURE that your product will work for them, and there is RISK associated with giving you money and spending their time and energy with you.

When you offer FREE services to them, you take away the entire money concern and can push a lot of people over the edge who ARE looking to buy but are just uncertain.

Offer FREE service to them.

And then follow the same playbook we talked about earlier:

1. Offer them free service.

2. Convert a percentage into paid service.

3. Give those people GREAT service so they stay.

4. Give those people GREAT service so those people tell other people (word of mouth).

5. Give those people GREAT service so you feel confident asking for referrals.

This next one is an add-on we didn't discuss regarding in-person coaching but could apply there as well, and it DEFINITELY applies to online:

6. Give those people GREAT service so you feel confident asking them for a TESTIMONIAL.

These testimonials you get from people using your service are what you can USE LATER in your posts and marketing to help show SOCIAL PROOF.

Before, we talked about the fact that people buy from people they KNOW, LIKE, and TRUST.

We discussed building TRUST with the audience by becoming a perceived expert through your content of HOW TO, DOCUMENTING, and STORYTELLING.

Well, one of the best add-ons to the storytelling or documenting part is to show testimonials—social proof.

When the audience sees people JUST LIKE THEM using your service and getting great results, it makes it easy for them to imagine themselves using your service and having success just like the person in your testimonial.

If they could do it, so could I!

So, you get your first set of customers in by:

1. Figuring out your offer (what you are selling).

2. Telling them about it (promotion/call to action).

3. Making it easy for them to buy (free/irresistible offer).

4. Giving that first set of customers EXCELLENT service/results.

5. Utilizing that first set of customers and their excellent results to encourage them to stay longer and increase their lifetime value.

6. Utilizing that first set of customers and their excellent results to get them to tell other people, get referrals, and provide testimonials to use in your content.

You see how this can start to build on itself, combined with the fact that you will KEEP ON talking about your offer, keep on posting, keep on getting new people, keep nurturing your current customers, and keep getting better at your craft.

This is the perfect storm of elements that can come together to build an online offer and business that can really change your life and your family's lives.

6. Craft an Irresistible Offer

"Make people an offer so good they would feel stupid saying no."

This is something I learned from Alex Hormozi in his book "$100M Offers." He quotes Trevor Jones, who said this to him during a business event when he asked Alex if he wanted to know the secret to sales.

Learning about and creating irresistible offers literally doubled and then tripled our monthly revenues on our membership site once I learned about them.

Some elements of an irresistible offer from my perspective:

1. Sell them the dream outcome they want (not the process).

2. Make them believe they are going to actually get it (proof/examples).

3. Within a reasonable time period (the shorter, the better).

4. Without crazy amounts of work (the less, the better).

5. Add a guarantee.

6. Add bonuses to 10X the value.

7. Include scarcity (only X number available) or urgency (offer ends by X) to push people over the edge.

This is so important to understand that I'll expand on it more in the next section.

The point here to grasp is that starting with FREE and following the sequence above will work GREAT, but there are some elements we can add to that offer to take it from GREAT to IRRESISTIBLE!

7. Focus as Much or More on Keeping Your Current Customers Than on Getting New Customers

I want to add this here just as a REMINDER and to maintain perspective.

We are talking a lot about how to get NEW or MORE customers, and don't get me wrong— to run and grow our businesses, we NEED to do that.

But in terms of ongoing revenue and predictable monthly income, we need to keep in mind that it is equally (if not more) important to be able to KEEP our current customers than it is to get new ones.

Remember, every customer who stays another month means one less NEW customer we need to acquire. If you need to get 10 customers to start at $100/month like I did to reach the first $1,000/month goal.

Well, what about the next month?

Would you rather have all those 10 leave and have to start over again to get 10 new people the next month? And the month after that, and after that...over and over again forever?

Or would you prefer that all those 10 people from the previous month stayed and automatically filled the next month's 10 spots without you needing to get anyone new?

Of course!

But not only does it make sense to auto-fill the spots and not have to sell to 10 new customers, what this also does is present us with an opportunity to control our supply and demand.

So, if those 10 people from month one want to stay for month two, great—we have our current 10 spots filled at the $1,000 price mark, and we are making our $1,000.

Now, we have a choice: we can adjust our supply (allow more than 10), say 15, 20, etc., to make more money,

OR

We can keep the supply the same (only 10 spots open), but since we will NOT STOP promoting our offer in our content (this is important to keep promoting even if you are full—this way, you get people who want your services on a WAITLIST for when spots open).

This creates more DEMAND: more people want our service than we have available spots. When a new spot opens up, we can increase our prices for new customers.For example, instead of charging $100 for the next group, we could raise it to $150, then $200, and so on.

We want to keep current customers for as long as possible, but of course, no matter how good we are, eventually people will leave, and new spots will open.

This is what I did in the early years. I filled my first 10 spots at $100 and made my $1,000 per month. I kept promoting it in my content and attracted more and more people who wanted to be on a "waiting list," instead of opening more slots (I was still doing my in-person coaching, creating content, etc., and didn't want to take on more people at that time).

So once a few people slowly left, new people would come in.

I went from $100 to $150 per month for the same service. Eventually, all my 10 were at my new price point, and I was making 10 people x $150/month = $1,500 per month.

Note: You can keep original/current customers at the same price ($100/month) and wait for them to leave and bring in new customers at $150, or you can raise your prices across the board for both NEW and existing customers. Just make sure if you do that, you are confident that you have NEW people ready to come in at the new price ($150) to make up for the $100 customers who leave.

I kept following this same process in the beginning. I kept my supply the same (10 spots open). I raised the demand (people who wanted those spots) by consistently posting content, making a call to action in all videos to promote the coaching offer, and building a waiting list.

Rise and repeat that process, and I went from $1,000 per month all the way to $5,000 per month!

I got 10 people in at $500 per month.

I underestimated what people were willing to pay per month when I started at $100 (too low), which helped the quick jump, but I followed the same steps above.

1. I first offered free to fill any empty spots.

2. I provided great service and went above and beyond to ensure they had success.

3. Because they liked the service, they told friends and family.

4. I asked them all for referrals.

5. I asked them all for testimonials and used them in my content.

6. I kept trying to make the offer better and more irresistible.

7. I kept my supply the same and kept increasing demand through content and promotion.

Now once I got to $5,000 per month and the process was working, combined with the dream life vision I was exposed to, I knew it was time to think bigger and scale my online business to greater heights.

Could I get this to $10,000 per month?

How about $30,000… $50,000… $100,000?

8. Scale Your Offer/Business

Once we start to see some initial success (and even before that), we want to think about HOW we can grow our coaching/services BEYOND just one-on-one coaching and beyond ourselves.

At some point, we will hit the same wall as we did with in-person coaching, which is that it's still US selling our time ONE-ON-ONE with just one person.

And we can definitely make more money doing that—we can build a SOLID business. But if we want more FREEDOM, more IMPACT, and to help MORE PEOPLE, we need to think bigger. Let's explore what some of those options look like.

9. Online Revenue Options Outside of 1-on-1 Coaching

If we stay focused just on revenue options and things we can do solely with our coaching/services, we have a few options to monetize our audience BEYOND our one-on-one coaching.

A) Membership Community

Building a membership site/community is what we decided to go with at www.cogornogolf.com, and that's what I would suggest for you.

Remember earlier when I was thinking about how I could get to that $100,000 per month mark I came up with during my dream life creation? Well, the options there were limited.

Schools or membership sites were really the only ways I could wrap my head around making $100,000 per month.

I looked around at what was currently in the market to model, and while there weren't a lot of people doing it at that time, I did see that the market rate was about $50/month for access to a membership site.

Now, the ones I saw were $50/month; you got access to their site, the videos, and some coaching from their coaches.

I thought, "OK, so at $50/month, we would need to get 2,000 people paying that amount per month."

Since I had ZERO at the time (but had sold a few people into that one-on-one monthly coaching program, as I mentioned above), I could actually wrap my head around it.

Looking back now, I would have charged MORE and aimed for closer to $100/month and getting 1,000 at that rate.

But I already knew I was close to maxed out with my in-person coaching and the 10 students I already had online, so the model needed to change.

1. We needed to go with a lower price point—low enough to sell the monthly price as a MEMBERSHIP model, NOT one-on-one for lessons.

2. We needed a model where they could post their swings for swing feedback, but that would just be part of the membership. They were no longer paying for the lesson; they were paying for ACCESS.

   - Access to be able to post swings.
   - Access to myself (and eventually other coaches) to ask questions.
   - Access to all of our videos in the member library.
   - Access to our masterclasses.
   - Access to our monthly live seminars.

So it was more like a gym model; they pay each month whether they use it or not.

If you don't go to the gym for a few weeks during the month, you don't get a discount or refund. In fact, if you don't go for a few months at a time but keep your membership, you continue paying—whether you use it or not.

This was really the only way I could think of at that time to reach that scale of $100,000 in revenue.

I also knew there was no way I could do that by myself, so I needed to add some coaches to help me with the lessons.

More on that next.

Think about how you could apply a membership model to your coaching.

Think BEYOND just a one-on-one exchange for a lesson or your time. Think more about a PACKAGE of services you could provide that would help them accomplish their goals and what you could charge for that.

When I first started, it was a bit more complicated, and we used sites like Thinkific, Kajabi, Facebook groups, etc., to build our membership site. Nowadays, there are a ton of "build for you" membership communities, like "SKOOL," for example, that you can use instead of having to build it yourself.

The community can help you SCALE your revenue for sure, as its main benefit. But just like I saw in those in-person group coaching sessions I mentioned, when people get into a community, they often LEARN better and STICK WITH YOU longer—they feel a part of something bigger.

It can work wonders when you get it right, and I would strongly recommend this option for you.

B) Course/Certification Program

We didn't go this route, but I know people who have had a lot of success building a "course" or "program" for people to go through.

This can be much more effective when you can teach the SAME concepts to EVERYONE.

With golf, for us, it was a bit more difficult in my opinion because I couldn't teach everyone the same thing; it needed to be highly personalized for their specific swing issues.

That said, I have still seen people in the golf space do this and launch successful "courses."

The benefit of this is that it can be a general program that everyone can follow. You can make a lot of money up front, and you don't need to provide individual service to everyone who joins.

The CON is that these courses usually require a lot of work upfront to create, and you only get paid once per person unless you upsell them into something else.

Not our expertise, but something to consider.

C) Group Coaching

You can do a form of group coaching with a community, but here I'm talking more about one-time or ongoing events.

For example, a webinar, where you present a topic and get as many people as you can to attend. This has the same sort of pros and cons as a course. The big pro here is you do something ONCE and can make a significant amount of money from it (or sell the recording or do more).

So, instead of doing a one-hour lesson with one person for $200 and making $200 total, maybe you do a one-hour webinar on a topic and charge $20. If you can get 20 people to sign up, you just made $400 and doubled your hourly rate.

Again, this is not something we really did, but it's something to consider.

10. Build A Team

As mentioned, when we started to create our membership site and I transitioned from thinking about 10 customers per month to 2,000 customers per month, I knew we would need help.

In the beginning, Mary and I did everything. We made the promotions, pitched the offer in the videos, I did all the coaching, we managed the site, and handled all the customer service, etc.

That works when the business is small, but sooner or later, if you follow the steps above, you will have more than just YOU can handle.

When looking to hire, I would hire people FIRST to help you with the tasks you can't do, don't like to do, aren't good at doing, or tasks that earn you less money per hour than your coaching.

You want to ensure that you keep doing WHAT YOU DO as much as you can for as long as you can.

It's the thing that will bring in the most amount of money — both for you and the team as a whole.

If you make $100 per hour coaching and are doing tasks you could pay someone $10 per hour to do, it doesn't make sense for you to do them.

You can start to buy back your time this way. For every $100 you make during a coaching hour, you could pay for 10 hours of someone at $10/hour to help manage the other tasks.

So keep that in mind; if you are spending even ONE hour doing a $10/hour task when you could be making $100 in that hour coaching, you are literally losing out on 10 hours you could be paying for.

With that in mind, I would hire in this order, assuming you have what you need to create good ongoing content:

A) Assistant

- Someone to handle those tasks to allow you to focus on coaching. Think answering calls, texts, emails, customer service, etc.

I worked with two different assistants while I was growing my in-person coaching and starting the online videos. Both were good, but eventually didn't work out for various reasons.

Later on, I received a cold email from a guy named Mikah, who enjoyed our videos and was interested in coming to work for us. I was lucky enough to find a GREAT assistant.

Don't give up if your first one isn't GREAT. Keep working at it, because when you find one that is, it can be a life changer!

B) Other Coaches

- Once you reach the point where your schedule is FULL and you don't have any more hours left in your day to fill with coaching—after already having an assistant and offloading all those tasks and focusing ONLY on the coaching (and making content/sales) side of things—then it's time to find other COACHES or people to help deliver your coaching/services.

We were lucky here to be early to market in 2017/2018 when we were building this, as not many people had online golf membership sites, and not a lot of coaches were doing online coaching.

So we really had the pick of the litter. I knew A LOT of great coaches in the coaching world from shadowing people, to the online groups, and attending events like I mentioned earlier.

Just like that awesome assistant who reached out to me, so did our first coaches.

First, my coaching friend JT reached out to see if we needed help, and we hired him.Then another coaching friend, Steve, reached out the same way, and we hired him.Next came Dennis, who also joined the team. So, our first three coaches all came from peers reaching out to us; that was great.

As we continued to grow, I did a little recruiting and asked those guys if they knew anyone who would be great. That led us to hiring another Steve and Andy.

We hired and worked with 2-3 other coaches along the way as well, but our core five have been with us now through most of our journey.

If you're looking to hire other coaches to deliver your coaching or service, you want to start at the TOP and try to get GREAT coaches.

Again, we got really lucky. These were guys who were just as good, if not better, than I was at coaching. We just happened to get an early start, be online doing the videos early, and built something that started to gain momentum.

So, there wasn't any training required. I didn't need to teach them to teach; they were already world-class.

This gave us a huge advantage because now we didn't just have ME; we had SIX world-class coaches.

Going back to the beginning, what does that mean?

That means great service/results for the members, them telling people about it, us asking for referrals, testimonials...the cycle continued.

We are still working on reaching 2,000, but with that cycle, we went from having those first 10 customers to over 1,500 customers every month!

C. Sales/Marketing

Hiring people to help with sales is likely more suited for those who choose to go the PAID route to grow your audience.

Using things like paid ads to attract people to a landing page and book a call with you or a sales rep to sell them your coaching is typically a bit higher ticket item (think $1,000+). However, if you can do it, whether paid or organic, to the point where you can have someone handle sales for you and figure out a commission rate that works for both parties, that would be a GREAT addition to your business.

Keep YOU focused on what YOU do (coaching) and hire people around you to help fill the gaps.

As for marketing, whether it be an individual or agency, it's worth investing in someone who can help you with your social media/marketing to throw fuel on the fire.

There are A LOT of options these days, so I would tread carefully here and make sure it makes sense for you and that they have a lot of credibility from other customers like you.

CHAPTER 13

Craft An Irresistible Offer

These are the elements and cliff notes of what I learned from Alex Hormozi in his book "$100M Offers." I can't recommend that you read this book enough.

I learned enough the first time I read it to launch new offers and take what I learned that led to us doubling and tripling our membership site revenue. It's powerful. I've since reread it about 10 more times as a refresher and learn something new each time.

Here are the elements I would consider to craft your irresistible offer.

Remember, our goal here is to "create an offer so good they would feel stupid saying no."

Think about that—brainstorm on that. How could you apply this to your business in your coaching/services offer? Use these as a guide.

You can go to www.acquisition.com (Alex's site) to see the value equation and all of his training materials!

1. Sell Them the Dream Outcome They Want, Not the Process

This is a big one I had to learn OVER AND OVER again for YEARS.

Sell them the OUTCOME they want, NOT THE PROCESS.

As one of the examples Alex discusses, if you are a travel agent selling someone a vacation trip somewhere, you want to sell them THE VACATION, not the trip there.

The time on the beach, the toes in the sand, the margaritas, the not having a care in the world, the sunshine, the ocean breeze… THAT is the outcome they really want. That's the FEELING they can imagine that will EVOKE EMOTION to move them to buy.

What we don't want to sell them or be talking about is the trip there—the car ride to the airport, the 6-hour flight, having to wait to get their bags, the car ride to the hotel, having to unload everything in the hotel, etc.

See the difference there?

We aren't selling them WHAT WE ARE GIVING THEM TO GET THERE; we are selling them WHERE THEY ARE GOING: THE DREAM OUTCOME!

So when we are crafting our offer, we want to have a REALLY GOOD IDEA of where our target customer WANTS TO GO.

What is their dream outcome? What do they want and why? Like, really, why?

Remember how important it was to ask those questions at the beginning of the in-person lessons and in the free trials to convert to paid?

That's because of this—and it works the same online.

If we can't directly ask them, we should have a good sense from current and former customers. We should know what our target customers really want.

EVERYONE wants the beach body at the end of the workout program; no one wants the 60 minutes of workouts for 12 weeks and a strict diet to get there.

So don't focus on that; focus on what they will look like AFTER the program—how good they will look, how good they will feel, how other people will compliment them, wondering how they did it, etc.

2. Make Them Believe They Are Going to Actually Get It (Proof/Examples)

So we already covered the dream outcome part; now we move on to the "perceived likelihood of achievement."

How likely do they think they are to actually get their dream outcome with you selling them what you are offering?

The higher the chance they think they will succeed, the higher the odds of them buying.

Remember, people buy from people they KNOW, LIKE, and TRUST.

We talked about building TRUST by showing PROOF — proof of yourself in your content and demonstrating expertise, as well as showing PROOF of results with your students, testimonials, and SOCIAL PROOF. That's big here.

You want to reiterate your expertise: how you've been coaching for X years, how you've worked with X thousands of students just like them who have achieved great results. It's helpful to say something like, "Here, check out _____ (testimonial of students) and the awesome results they got with our _____ program."

The more they see other people like them succeeding with your service, the more they will believe they can do it too.

3. Within a Reasonable Time Period (the Shorter the Better)

Now we are at the "time delay" part.

For the first two parts of this (dream outcome and perceived likelihood of achievement), we want to INCREASE.

On the bottom of the equation, we want to DECREASE.

The SOONER they can achieve the results (dream outcome) you are selling them, the higher the chance of the sale and the more irresistible the offer.

Imagine you buy something and you have to wait 6 months to get it in the mail.

How likely are you to buy that?

How about if you buy it and immediately your doorbell rings and it's delivered?

Are you more likely to buy it when you receive it immediately or when you have to wait 6 months?

Obviously, the immediate option.

This also affects the price point you can charge, but in terms of making the offer so good that they feel stupid saying no, the sooner we can deliver RESULTS and WINS, the more likely they are to buy.

Now, of course, this needs to be within reason.

If you are selling a weight loss program where the goal is to lose 30 pounds, we can't say they are going to do that by the next day.

So even if they can't get the FINAL result right away, we can sell IMPROVEMENT right away.

They aren't going to lose 30 pounds tomorrow, but they can start losing it right away, feeling better right away, looking better right away, etc. ALONG THE WAY.

The less time to the results, the more irresistible the offer.

4. Without Crazy Amounts of Work (the Less, the Better)

Part 4 is Effort and Sacrifice. Again, on the bottom of the equation, we want to DECREASE this.

The LESS WORK they need to do to get the dream outcome, the easier the sale.

The MORE WORK they need to do to get the dream outcome, the more difficult the sale.

Keep in mind that when we are discussing our offer, we are NOT GOING TO FOCUS ON THE WORK; we are going to focus on the outcome they want and how they can imagine themselves there.

Just remember when talking about this that it works the same as the time delay. We know that to get the results, they are going to need to do SOMETHING—SOME WORK.

They need to believe it's an amount of work they can manage without any issues, but the EASIER we can make it for them, the better the offer.

5. Add a Guarantee (REVERSE RISK)

One of the biggest reasons people don't buy is because of RISK.

At the end of the day, if they are exchanging money with you to get a desired result, there is always RISK—no matter what we say or do.

To get someone to buy so we can deliver the service they need to achieve their dream outcome, we want to REDUCE or ELIMINATE that risk as much as possible.

You can do this with a guarantee.

Alex discusses this in detail in his book, but essentially what we are doing here is either guaranteeing results or guaranteeing their money back if they don't get the results.

There are A LOT of clever ways you can go about this, as he talks through, but some simple options you can start with would be:

- A money-back guarantee (if they don't get results or like the service, they get their money back). You can add a timeframe here, like 30, 60, or 90 days.

- A results-backed guarantee (you will keep working with them until they achieve the agreed-upon desired result, even after they stop paying).

Offering a FREE trial can take care of a lot of this if you choose that route; there is nothing less risky than FREE. They get to TRY before they BUY—the only thing they are risking is their time and energy, but no money. This will help push A LOT of people over the edge.

6. Add Bonuses to 10X the Value

Just like the PERCEIVED Likelihood of achieving the goal will affect the odds of them buying, so will the PERCEIVED VALUE of the offer.

When someone FEELS like they are getting a DEAL, they are more likely to buy.

When they FEEL like they are getting WAY more than they are paying for, they are in.

We can do this by STACKING BONUSES to the offer.

Usually, a good marker to shoot for that I learned from Russell Brunson is to be in the 10x range. That means including bonuses (and the values of those bonuses) that add up to 10 times the actual price of the program.

Here's an example WITHOUT BONUSES:

A) Online Coaching

- One-hour lesson with Eric
- Total Value: $100
- Cost: $100

B) VIP Online Coaching Gold Plan

- One-hour lesson with Eric ($100 value)
- Ultimate Ball Striking Masterclass ($200 value)
- All 10 "Transform Your Swing" Live Seminar Series ($200 value)
- Unlimited Q&A with coaches throughout the month ($100 value)
- Exclusive Member Community Access for accountability and encouragement ($100 value)
- Pro Level Club Fitting Template to ensure your equipment is perfect for you ($200 value)
- Member Library (over 200 videos) plus full practice plans ($100 value)

Total Value: $1,000

Cost: $100

You see the difference here?

Are you more likely to buy option A or option B?

Which one FEELS like you are getting a better DEAL?

The PERCEIVED value being 10x higher will move the needle and have more people feel stupid saying no.

7. Include Scarcity (Only X # Available) or Urgency (Offer Ends by X) to Get People Over the Edge

These factors have been game changers for our business since we included this specific strategy to push more and more people over the edge to buy, especially at the "END" of the sale.

I've found we make around 80% of our sales on the FIRST and LAST day of the sale.

So, let's say we do a 7-day sales offer.

Around 80% of those sales will happen on day 1 and day 7.

20% will happen between day 2 and day 6.

That's just human nature.

To take advantage of this, we want to add URGENCY (timing) or SCARCITY (amount).

Scarcity moves people to act.

When there are only a LIMITED amount available, if it's something they are interested in, they are MORE LIKELY TO BUY if they FEEL like they might MISS OUT on it.

So, when you sell something, you might say, "We are only offering _____ spots. Once they are gone, they are gone. First come, first serve." I've used this strategy repeatedly to fill both in-person and online coaching offers.

The other option is URGENCY, which is a time-based constraint. The offer is only valid until X day. Again, tapping into the procrastination we all have and putting a DEADLINE makes people act.

Think about in school when we had a paper or project due at a certain time. We would suddenly get really creative and figure things out out of nowhere during those last hours. The same thing happens with a sale. Use these strategies to your advantage.

Remember, at the end of the day, we have a coaching/service that WE TRULY BELIEVE will help them—will help them achieve their goals and accomplish their dream outcome. SO IF WE REALLY BELIEVE IN THAT, it's our duty to do EVERYTHING we can to get them to buy so we can help them.

If not, they are just going to keep being stuck doing what they are doing and never improve—and our business never grows. No one wants either of those outcomes.

HOW WE USED THESE

While we have tested a bunch of variations of offers over the years, some of the core elements have stayed the same.

Here is an example of how we would use this to sell our online membership using our 14-day Free Trial to help golfers.

1. Sell Them the Dream Outcome

I would say something like:

"This program is designed to get you hitting the ball better fast. Hit it solid day in and day out, with a swing that you can rely on. Imagine playing golf with a swing that feels SMOOTH and EFFORTLESS. Picture that flush contact you're going to be making on each shot—hitting your drives LONG and STRAIGHT and shooting the best scores of your life.

That's what I'm here to do for you."

2. Make Them Believe They Are Actually Going To Get It

I would say something like:

"Hey, my name's Eric Cogorno, if you don't already know me. I've been coaching golf for the past 15 years, both in person and online. I've been lucky enough to be featured in FORBES for our innovative online coaching and have been voted a BEST TEACHER IN STATE in Golf Digest. I've given over 20,000 lessons, with over 10,000 of those being completely online. The results have been amazing. Just take a look at some of these players (show testimonials or before and afters)."

(This would be more for an audience who doesn't know me and hasn't watched our content.)

For those who already watch our content:

"Guys, you hear me say all the time that if we could SEE YOUR SWING, we could REALLY help take your game to the next level. And that's exactly what I want to do for you at www.cogornogolf.com.

We've helped over 10,000 students to date and the results have been awesome (show testimonials/before and afters)."

3. + 4. Within a Reasonable Period of Time

I would say something like:

"You're going to get results FAST. I've seen so many transformations in the first month. The key is, when you find the RIGHT root cause and fix it the RIGHT way, you can address your issues FAST. You don't need to hit balls for hours on the range; I'm talking as little as 20-30 swings a few days per week!"

5. Add a Guarantee

I would say something like:

"Best of all, you get to try all of this BEFORE you buy with our 14-day free trial. I'm going to personally analyze your swing, diagnose the issues, and show you how to fix those fast. And you pay NOTHING.

Watch the analysis, and if you like it, we can talk about working together. If not, no harm, no foul. You pay nothing and get to KEEP the analysis as my gift to you and my thanks for supporting us!"

6. Add Bonuses

I would add that same stack as above.

7. Include Scarcity or Urgency

I would say something like:

"This offer is only available for the first 20 people who sign up, or this offer is only available until November 15th, and then it's gone!"

CHAPTER 14

Conclusion

There we have it.

Hopefully, you've enjoyed learning more about my journey and discovered a bunch of real-life tactical things you can use to help grow and optimize your own coaching/services business.

None of this stuff is EASY; there are no TRICKS. But all of the above is what I actually did that WORKED.

If you're like me, you don't mind putting in the work if you know you're doing the RIGHT WORK to help you grow and improve.

We could probably do a full book on each chapter above, even on each micro topic, but I wanted to give you a more BROAD STROKES, MACRO look at everything first to paint a picture of what things can look like as you build your business and dream lifestyle.

Thank you for your time and support. If you have any questions or ever need anything, please feel free to reach out to me at eric@cogornogolf.com, and I'd love to help!